Foreign Trade and
Export-Import Policy of India

By
Madhusudana H.S.
Associate Professor and Head,
Department of Economics,
Government First Grade College, Mulbagal, Kolar, Karnataka

New Century Publications
New Delhi, India

NEW CENTURY PUBLICATIONS
4852 / 24, 1st Floor,
Ansari Road, Daryaganj,
New Delhi – 110 002 (India)

Tel.: 011-4101 7798; 4358 7398; 98112 66355
E-mail: info@newcenturypublications.com

www.newcenturypublications.com

Editorial office:
4800 / 24, Bharat Ram Road,
Ansari Road, Daryaganj,
New Delhi – 110 002

Reprint: 2024

ISBN: **978-81-7708-501-3**

First Published: 2020

Published by New Century Publications and printed at Milan Enterprises, New Delhi.

Designs: Patch Creative Unit, New Delhi.

PRINTED IN INDIA

About the Book

Between 1950 and 1990, foreign trade of India suffered from strict bureaucratic and discretionary controls. Beginning 1991, the Government of India introduced a series of reforms to liberalise and globalise the Indian economy. Reforms in the foreign trade sector were intended to integrate Indian economy with the global economy. The major trade policy changes in the post-1991 period have included simplification of procedures, removal of quantitative restrictions, and substantial reduction in the tariff rates.

Since early 1990s, India's foreign trade has undergone a complete change in terms of composition and direction. Exports now cover a wide range of traditional and non-traditional items while imports mainly consist of capital goods, petroleum products, raw materials, and chemicals to meet the ever-increasing needs of a developing and diversifying economy.

Exports have acquired added significance in the wake of liberalisation wave sweeping across the world. The trend towards market economy in almost all the countries of the world has increased the role of exports in developmental efforts. Exports have become an important indicator of a country's economic performance.

The surge in exports has provided a strong stimulus to domestic industrial growth. While software exports are a well-known success story, India is now an important venue for many tasks in services such as financial accounting, call centres, processing insurance claims, and medical transcription. The future potential for growth in these areas appears to be considerable.

The process of opening up of the Indian economy has given birth to a host of new challenges and opportunities. The spirit of the liberalisation process entails a conscious effort on the part of policy makers to optimise on these opportunities-challenges trade-offs.

About the Author

Dr. Madhusudana H.S. is presently Associate Professor and Head, Department of Economics, Government First Grade College, Mulbagal, Kolar District, Karnataka. He obtained his M.A. (Economics) and M.Phil. degrees from Bangalore University, Bangalore in 1993 and 1996 respectively. He received his Ph.D. degree from Sri Krishnadevaraya University, Ananthapuramu, Andhra Pradesh in 2005. He has participated and presented research papers at various national and international conferences. He has visited University of Malaysia and University of Singapore as a resource person. He has to his credit more than 25 publications in national and 20 publications in international peer-reviewed journals of repute.

He has also published 5 books on various aspects of the Indian economy, namely *Rural Development and Poverty Alleviation in India* (2012), *Indian Economy towards Inclusive Growth* (2013), *Infrastructure Development and the Role of Public-Private-Partnership (PPP)* (2017), *Agricultural Crisis and Farmers-friendly Reforms in India* (2018) and *Foreign Direct Investment (FDI) and Ease of Doing Business in India* (2019).

Contents

Preface

India has been an important trading nation since ancient times. However, the restrictive policies of commodity production, trade and tariff pursued by British rulers adversely affected the structure, composition and volume of India's foreign trade. Consequently, India became an exporter of primary products such as raw silk, cotton, wool, sugar, indigo, jute etc. and an importer of finished consumer goods like cotton, silk and woollen clothes and capital goods like light machinery produced in the factories of Britain. For all practical purposes, Britain maintained a monopoly control over India's exports and imports. As a result, more than half of India's foreign trade was restricted to Britain while the rest was allowed with a few other countries like China, Ceylon (now Sri Lanka) and Persia (now Iran).

Since Independence in 1947, India's foreign trade has undergone a complete change in terms of composition and direction. Exports now cover a wide range of traditional and non-traditional items while imports mainly consist of capital goods, petroleum products, raw materials, and chemicals to meet the ever-increasing needs of a developing and diversifying economy.

Exports have acquired added significance in the wake of liberalisation wave sweeping across the world. The trend towards market economy in almost all the countries of the world has increased the role of exports in developmental efforts. Exports have become an important indicator of a country's economic performance.

India's approach to openness has been cautious, contingent on achieving certain preconditions to ensure an orderly process of liberalisation and ensuring macroeconomic stability.

Department of Commerce, Ministry of Commerce and Industry, Government of India is the nodal agency for the regulation, development and promotion of India's international trade and commerce. Goals are realized through the formulation of appropriate international trade and commercial policy and its effective implementation.

The products wherein India has the maximum presence in international market in terms of export share are spices, marine products, precious and semi-precious stones, textiles. Recent trends, however, indicate that the commodity structure of India's exports has slowly begun to shift towards higher technology-intensive manufactures.

The sustained buoyancy in the export of gems and jewellery reflects the effects of continuing policy initiatives. The Government of India and the Gem and Jewellery Export Promotion Council (GJEPC), a representative body of the trade, have taken several steps to improve exports of gems and jewellery and enhance competitiveness.

It is expected that the future export drivers for India will be textiles, engineering goods, including automobiles and capital goods and processed food items. Textiles have long been a traditional export item for India accounting for nearly one-fifth of the total exports during the 1990s.

The greatest challenge facing the Indian economy is to enhance its productivity and competitiveness so as to achieve a sustained growth in exports of goods and services.

Kolar **Madhusudana H.S.**

June 2020

Trade-related Abbreviations/Acronyms

ACU	Asian Clearing Union
ADB	African Development Bank
AEPC	Apparel Export Promotion Council
AEZs	Agricultural Export Zones
AID	Agency for International Development (US)
AIMO	All India Manufacturers Organisation
APEDA	Agricultural and Processed Food Products Export Development Authority
ASEAN	Association of Southeast Asian Nations
ADB	Asian Development Bank
ASSOCHAM	Associated Chambers of Commerce and Industry of India
BG	Bank Guarantee
BIFR	Board for Industrial and Financial Reconstruction
BOA	Board of Approval
CACM	Central American Common Market
CAPEXIL	Chemicals and Allied Products Export Promotion Council
CCIC	Central Cottage Industries Corporation
CCP	Customs Clearance Permit
CEPC	Carpet Export Promotion Council
CEPCI	Cashew Export Promotion Council of India
CFS	Container Freight Stations
CIF	Cost, Insurance and Freight
CII	Confederation of Indian Industry
CIS	Commonwealth of Independent States
CLE	Council for Leather Exports
CoD	Cash on Delivery
CSB	Central Silk Board
CVD	Countervailing Duty
DEPB	Duty Entitlement Passbook Scheme
DFIA	Duty Free Import Authorisation
DFRC	Duty Free Replenishment Certificate

DGCI&S	Directorate General of Commercial Intelligence and Statistics
DGFT	Directorate General of Foreign Trade
DIPP	Department of Industrial Policy and Promotion
DoBT	Department of Bio-Technology
DTA	Domestic Tariff Area
ECGC	Export Credit Guarantee Corporation of India
ECSEPC	Electronics and Computer Software Export Promotion Council
EDI	Electronic Data Interchange
EHTP	Electronic Hardware Technology Park
EIC	Export Inspection Council
EOP	Export Obligation Period
EOU	Export Oriented Unit
EPC	Export Promotion Council
EPCG	Export Promotion of Capital Goods
EPO	Engineering Process Outsourcing
FASII	Federation of Associations of Small Industries of India
FDI	Foreign Direct Investment
FICCI	Federation of Indian Chambers of Commerce and Industry
FIEO	Federation of Indian Export Organisations
FIRC	Foreign Exchange Inward Remittance Certificate
FMS	Focus Market Scheme
FOB	Free on Board
FPS	Focus Product Scheme
FTDO	Foreign Trade Development Officer
GJEPC	Gem and Jewellery Export Promotion Council
GATS	General Agreement on Trade in Services
GATT	General Agreement on Tariffs and Trade
GDP	Gross Domestic Product
HEPC	Handloom Export Promotion Council

HHEC	Handicrafts and Handlooms Exports Corporation of India Ltd.
IBRD	International Bank for Reconstruction and Development (World Bank)
ICC	International Chamber of Commerce
ICD	Inland Container Depot
ICM	Indian Commercial Mission
IEC	Import-Export Code Number
IIC	Indian Investment Centre
IIFT	Indian Institute of Foreign Trade
IIP	Indian Institute of Packaging
IMF	International Monetary Fund
ISEPC	Indian Silk Export Promotion Council
ISO	International Standards Organisation
ITPO	India Trade Promotion Organisation
JCI	Jute Corporation of India Limited
JMCD	Jute Manufacturers Development Council
LoI	Letter of Intent
LoP	Letter of Permit
MAI	Market Assistance Initiative
MAI	Market Access Initiative
MDA	Market Development Assistance
MMTC	Metals and Minerals Trading Corporation of India
MPEDA	Marine Products Export Development Authority
MTC	Mica Trading Corporation
OCCI	Overseas Construction Council of India
OECD	Organisation for Economic Cooperation and Development
OPEC	Organization of the Petroleum Exporting Countries
RBI	Reserve Bank of India
SAARC	South Asian Association for Regional Cooperation
SEH	Star Export House

SEZ	Special Economic Zone
SFIS	Served from India Scheme
SGEPC	Sports Goods Export Promotion Council
SIA	Secretariat for Industrial Assistance
SIL	Special Imprest Licence
SMEs	Small and Medium-Sized Enterprises
SOPA	Soybean Processors Association of India
SREPC	Synthetic and Rayon Textiles Export Promotion Council
SSI	Small-scale Industry
STC	State Trading Corporation of India Ltd.
STE	State Trading Enterprise
STH	Star Trading House
STP	Software Technology Park
TEXPROCIL	Cotton Textiles Export Promotion Council of India
TRQ	Tariff Rate Quota
UNCTAD	United Nations Conference on Trade and Development
UNDP	United Nations Development Programme
UNEP	United Nations Environment Programme
USAID	United States Agency for International Development
VAT	Value-added Tax
WEU	Western European Union
WTO	World Trade Organization
WWEPC	Wool and Woollens Export Promotion Council

Conversion Table

Unit Conversion

1 lakh = 0.1 million
10 lakh = 1.0 million
1 crore = 10.0 million
100 crore = 1.0 billion

Exchange Rate

The unit of currency in India is Indian Rupee, symbolized as ₹. As per reference rate of Reserve Bank of India (RBI) for June 2, 2020

US$ 1 = ₹ 75.58
UK£ 1 = ₹ 94.63
Euro (€) 1 = ₹ 84.11

Fiscal Year

Fiscal year in India runs from April 1 to March 31 of the following year.

Pre- and Post-metric Systems of Currency in India

Metric system of currency in India was introduced from April 1, 1957

In the pre-metric system, one Rupee was = 16 *annas* and one *anna* was = 4 paise

In the post-metric system, one Rupee = 100 paise

1

Pre-Independence Foreign Trade

India's foreign trade started assuming significance during the latter half of the 19th century due to: (a) opening of the Suez Canal, (b) industrial revolution in Europe, (c) expansion of the Indian railway system and (d) restoration of peace and order by the British following the decline of the Mughal Empire.

1.1 India's Foreign Trade in Ancient Times

India has been a global trader for centuries, and there is evidence of India's trading with the different countries of Europe in the West and the lands to the East up to China in ancient times. Evidences of Indian goods reaching far away lands in those days, as well as foreign goods landing in Indian ports, reflect the spirit of enterprise of Indians which has remained undiminished, despite the political and social strife that the country saw on a massive scale across centuries.

Commerce in India is recorded as far back as 3,500 B.C. when a fairly large-scale agricultural economy was existing in the main river basin areas, spreading gradually over the next 3,000 years to all parts of the sub-continent. Thc Archaeological excavations carried out during the 1920s and 1930s at Mohenjo-daro and Harappa (both now in Pakistan) and excavations at Rangpur (in Gujarat) clearly indicate that well before 1,500 B.C. Indians were carrying on trade with far-off lands with West Asia and beyond

The most important feature of India's foreign trade was that India always had a surplus with the whole world including Europe, which was settled by the inflow of gold into India.

1.2 Favourable Balance of Trade during 17th Century

The demand for Indian goods in Europe was great in the

17th century due to the exploits of European companies. Since the demand for European goods in India was limited, the balance of trade always remained in favour of India. In spite of the restrictions imposed by several European governments against the export of bullion from their respective countries, these companies had to import treasures into India to finance their operations. The British government revised its customs regulations in 1700 and then in 1720 to discourage the use of Indian textile goods in Britain. The activities of the Europeans resulted in net economic gain to India and a large portion of these gains went to the mercantile classes. The weavers, who used to manufacture the textile goods in which the Europeans were mainly interested, were too poor to finance their operations. They depended on the mercantile communities for capital who advanced funds under a system of contract which precluded any marginal profit accruing to the manufacturers. The mercantile communities used their gains to finance their traditional activities like trade and money lending.

The most important characteristic of India's foreign trade throughout the colonial period was the generation of a large export surplus. But this surplus came at a huge cost to the country's economy. Several essential commodities—foodgrains, clothes, kerosene etc.—were scarcely available in the domestic market. Furthermore, this export surplus did not result in any flow of gold or silver into India. Rather, this was used to make payments for *home charges* and imports of invisibles (i.e. services such as shipping and insurance provided by British companies). All this led to the drain of Indian wealth.

1.3 The Period 1857-1900

During British rule, foreign trade of India was typical of a colonial and agricultural economy. Trade relations were mainly confined to Britain and other Commonwealth countries. Exports consisted chiefly of raw materials and plantation crops while imports composed of light consumer goods and other manufactures. The structure of India's foreign trade reflected the systematic exploitation of the country by the foreign rulers. Cotton textiles, which at one time constituted the bulk of India's exports, accounted for the largest share of her imports during the British rule. Obviously, it resulted in the decay and decline of Indian industries.

India's foreign trade started assuming significance during the latter half of the 19th century. The important factors which stimulated foreign trade were the following.

1. Opening of the Suez Canal.
2. Industrial revolution in Europe.
3. Expansion of the Indian railway system.
4. Restoration of peace and order by the British following the decline of the Mughal Empire.

By and large, progress of India's foreign trade during 1857-1900 was unprecedented both in terms of volume and variety of goods traded. During 1894-1900, India's foreign trade received a temporary set back due to re-imposition of import duties in 1894, general trade depression abroad, famines and plague towards the close of 19th century.

The period 1900-1914 again witnessed remarkable expansion in India's foreign trade. It was a period of world-wide prosperity and favourable monsoons in the sub-continent. The rise in the output of such commercial crops as oilseeds, cotton, jute and tea was largely due to a flourishing export trade. This period also witnessed a remarkable change in the direction of India's foreign trade. The share of non-empire countries increased in India's exports and imports. Britain faced stiff competition from USA, Germany and Japan.

1.4 First World War

The first half of the 20th century witnessed many turbulent events. Beginning with the First World War, the problems during the inter-war period, the Great Depression (1929-34) and the Second World War, all of them disturbed the world economy. Most of the economies were directly or indirectly stricken badly by these events. During 1919 to 1939, Indian imports and exports showed a declining trend. Exports during the Second World War rose rapidly, the imports remaining more or less stagnant.

The First World War gave a serious set back to India's foreign trade. Many factors were responsible for the shrinkage of foreign trade during the war period. There was almost complete stoppage of trade with enemy countries. There were transport difficulties and movement of goods was risky due to blockades and similar enemy activities. In the immediate Post-war period (1919-1920), India's exports increased sharply due to increase in world demand for raw materials and the removal of war-time restrictions. Imports also increased to satisfy the pent-up demand. The recovery of India's foreign trade was attributable to a number of internal and external factors. These included the following:

1. Good monsoons for a number of years after 1922.
2. Stability of the rupee.
3. Return of economic and political normalcy to Europe.
4. Stabilisation of international currencies.

However, in the next two years imports started declining due to *Swadeshi* movement, and increase in import tariff in 1922-23.

1.5 Great Depression

India's foreign trade was severely hit by the Great Depression. The value of total trade in 1932-33 was less than half of that in 1929-30. The decline was sudden and continuous both in exports and imports. The decline in the value of exports was due to the following reasons:

1. Steep fall in the prices of agricultural products.
2. Decline in the demand for India's staples.

The value of imports declined due to the following factors:

1. Reduced purchasing power of the consumers in India.
2. Tense political situation in the country.
3. Expansion of domestic sugar and cotton textile industries under the policy of discriminating protection.

Before the war, India was a net debtor country and had to have a surplus of a fairly large order in its trade accounts in order to meet the servicing charges on the sterling debt. This was therefore the key to its commercial policy. In the wider pattern of international balance of payments, India was among the group of countries which were net dollar earners and made over those earnings to the metropolitan countries of Europe in payment for the deficits which they had with them. It was a member of the sterling area, one of the main objectives of which was to expand trade within the area while preserving the stability of sterling as an international currency.

Under the conditions that prevailed in the 1930s, this meant that a certain measure of discrimination in trade was unavoidable. In so far as the discriminatory principle was implicit in arrangements like Imperial Preference, it was an important factor which also affected commercial policy.

The impact of depression began to subside after 1932 and India's foreign trade showed signs of improvement. In spite of an upward trend, India's foreign trade in the post-depression period did not regain the glory of pre-depression period.

1.6 Second World War

In May 1940, import restrictions were imposed for the first time on the import of consumer goods and the control was later gradually extended to almost all commodities by the end of January 1942. The sole objective of this measure at that point of time was to regulate available foreign exchange and the limited shipping space available for the war effort and for essential civilian supplies. During the Second World War, India experienced huge export surplus, enabling her to accumulate substantial amounts of sterling balances.

During the War, there was a basic change in the nature of India's foreign trade as the British Government commandeered from poverty-stricken people of India huge supplies of foodstuffs leather-ware, iron and steel etc. for the prosecution of the War. There was a favourable balance of trade with Britain.

By the end of the war, almost the entire external debt of the Government was repaid and balances of the order of ₹ 1,600 crore had been built up in sterling. This obviated the necessity for having a surplus on trade account. The magnitude of the external reserves accumulated during the war opened up in fact the prospect of being able to finance fairly large deficits in balance of payments. However, the post-war difficulties of the United Kingdom placed a limit on the rate at which the sterling balances could be drawn upon.

Since the sterling balances were largely the result of restricted consumption and investment and not a reflection of any permanent improvement in productivity in the economy, the problem of balancing trade at the end of the war was in a sense more difficult than before it. The financing of the war had increased money incomes but consumption had been kept down by scarcities and price rises. In industry and transport there had been not only little net addition to capital equipment during the war but even normal depreciation requirements had to be postponed. On the conclusion of the war, the economy was in a starved condition, and it was necessary to provide for imports on a large scale to make good the results of war-time austerity and depletion of capital, not to mention the needs of development.

Even apart from the pressure of pent up demand, the import requirements were larger and exportable surpluses smaller at the end of the war. This was on account of the increase in population in the interval and the partition of the country which enlarged the country's deficit in food and raw materials. Changes necessitated by wartime requirements in the pattern of production also aggravated the difficulty. These changes were responsible for a sharp contraction in the exportable surpluses of staple commodities like raw cotton and raw jute. Oilseeds and pig iron were also required in large quantities to meet increased domestic industrial needs. The decline in the exports of these commodities was to some extent counter-balanced by increased exports of primary products like spices and mica and of semi-manufactures such as vegetable oil, but the volume of exports in 1946-47 was still only about two-thirds of the pre-war level.

There were two further developments in this period which were significant from the point of view of commercial policy, one relating to the composition of exports and the other to the direction of trade.

In 1938-39, jute manufactures, cotton manufactures and tea accounted for only about 35 percent of the total value of India's exports. Of the rest, raw cotton, raw jute, oilseeds, hides and skins, metals and ores and raw wool contributed as much as 40 percent. In the following decade this distribution became much more uneven. By 1948-49, the share of jute and cotton manufactures and tea had risen to over 56 percent, while the contribution of the latter group fell to less than 15 percent. The increased dependence on a few commodities not only introduced an element of instability in export prospects but was bound to weaken the country's position in regard to larger questions of policy.

Before the war, over half of India's foreign trade was with countries which constituted the sterling area, only about 10 percent on average was with the dollar area, while the rest was distributed between a number of countries in Europe, the Middle East and the Far East which did not fall in either of these groups. During the Second War, exports increased rapidly, particularly to Britain, as compared to imports. This resulted into a favourable balance of trade. Britain and USA accounted for the bulk of India's exports. During the war, trade with Japan and Germany, Britain's enemy countries, completely disappeared. After the War, the share of the sterling area became somewhat smaller. Trade with Germany and Japan also declined sharply. Resultantly, there was an increase in the share of the dollar area to about a quarter of the country's total foreign trade.

On the side of exports there was no significant compositional change in the trade with the dollar area, except that new commodities like cashew nuts, manganese ore, and spices assured greater importance as dollar earners. However, the pattern of imports changed considerably in this period, mainly on account of the greater dependence on this area for supplies of foodgrains and developmental commodities.

1.7 Post-War Period

Meanwhile, the period between the end of the War and Independence saw some liberalisation of imports. The new policy on import trade control introduced in July 1947 freed the import of food, capital goods, and certain raw materials required by industries as well as certain essential consumer goods. There was also a list of restricted items and a list of prohibited items, the banned list being made up of luxury items numbering over 200. The distinction between imports from the sterling area and the general currency area was by and large removed (except for a differential tariff). A noteworthy feature of the new import control system was a change-over to a system of quantum licensing, based on exchange ceilings allowed for the import of specific commodities.

The partition of the country resulted in most of the areas growing food, raw cotton and raw jute going to Pakistan, while cotton and jute manufacturing industries were located in India. Besides food, India had, therefore, to import raw cotton and raw jute on a large scale. The resultant heavy import bill impinged on the foreign exchange position and led to more and thorough screening of import items.

Partition affected most the exports of jute, cotton, and hides. In the new set-up, large scale imports of these were essential for some of the largest established industries in India. But the commodities that could be exported to Pakistan in exchange were mainly processed materials like cotton textiles, sugar, and matches which, until Partition, were receiving some protection against foreign competition in the areas which now constitute Pakistan. Partition therefore not only resulted in increased reliance on imported raw materials but made more difficult the problem of export promotion.

To sum up, India has been an important trading nation since ancient times. However, the restrictive policies of commodity production, trade and tariff pursued by the colonial government adversely affected the structure, composition and volume of India's foreign trade. Consequently, India became an exporter of primary products such as raw silk, cotton, wool, sugar, indigo, jute etc. and an importer of finished consumer goods like cotton, silk and woollen clothes and capital goods like light machinery produced in the factories of Britain. For all practical purposes, Britain maintained a monopoly control over India's exports and imports. As a result, more than half of India's foreign trade was restricted to Britain while the rest was allowed with a few other countries like China, Ceylon (now Sri Lanka) and Persia (now Iran).

The opening of the Suez Canal further intensified British control over India's foreign trade. By and large, India enjoyed export surplus in its foreign trade during the last one hundred years of British rule. But the continued surplus in balance of trade did not mean any real gain for it as it was used to pay for invisible imports and debt servicing obligations. In fact, the favourable balance of trade was accompanied by net import of capital after 1850. This contradiction could be explained in terms of invisible items and the unilateral transfer of fund to Britain as *political charges*. Thus, the payment of *political tribute* was the genesis of the famous theory of *drain of wealth* from India.

2

Legal and Institutional Framework for Foreign Trade

2.1 Constitutional Provisions and the Law

In the federal polity of India, foreign trade is a Central subject. Entry 41 of List I (Union List) of the Seventh Schedule of the Constitution of India states the powers of the Central Government in matters related to "trade and commerce with foreign countries, import and export across customs frontiers, definition of customs frontiers". Further, Entry 51 of the same list provides for, "establishment of standards of quality for goods to be exported out of India or transported from one State to another".

Foreign trade of India is regulated by the Foreign Trade (Development and Regulation) Act, 1992 which replaced the Import and Export (Control) Act, 1947. The Act of 1992 empowers the Central Government to formulate and announce from time to time the export and import policy and to amend it in like manner.

Another significant legislation is the Special Economic Zones Act, 2005, which was passed by Parliament in May 2005. Supported by SEZ Rules, it came into effect on February 10, 2006, providing for drastic simplification of procedures and for single window clearance on matters relating to Central as well as State Governments. For more details, see chapter 10 of this book.

Other important Acts regulating foreign trade are as under:

1. Marine Products Export Development Authority (MPEDA) Act, 1972.
2. Export Quality Control and Inspection Act, 1963.
3. Coffee Board Act, 1942.

4. Tea Board Act, 1953.
5. Spices Board Act, 1986.
6. Tobacco Board Act, 1975
7. Rubber Board Act, 1947.

2.2 Department of Commerce, Ministry of Commerce and Industry

The mandate of the Department of Commerce, Ministry of Commerce and Industry, Government of India is regulation, development and promotion of India's international trade and commerce. Goals are realized through the formulation of appropriate international trade and commercial policy and its effective implementation. The long-term vision is to make India a major player in world trade by 2020, and assume a role of leadership in international trade organizations commensurate with India's growing importance.

The Department formulates, implements and monitors the Foreign Trade Policy which provides the basic framework of policy and strategy to be followed for promoting exports and trade. Foreign Trade Policy is periodically reviewed to incorporate changes necessary to take care of emerging economic scenarios, both in the domestic and international economy. Besides, the Department is also entrusted with responsibilities relating to multilateral and bilateral commercial relations, special economic zones (SEZs), state trading, export promotion and trade facilitation, and development and regulation of certain export-oriented industries and commodities.

The basic role of the Department is to facilitate the creation of an enabling environment and infrastructure for accelerated growth of international trade.

2.3 Attached Offices of the Department of Commerce

These are as under:

2.3.1 Directorate General of Foreign Trade (DGFT): Directorate General of Foreign Trade (DGFT) organisation is an attached office of the Ministry of Commerce and Industry and is headed by Director General of Foreign Trade. Right from its inception till 1991, when liberalization in the economic policies of the Government took place, this organization has been essentially involved in the regulation and promotion of foreign trade through regulation. Keeping in line with liberalization and globalization and the overall objective of increasing of exports, DGFT has since been assigned the role of *facilitator*. The shift was from prohibition and control of imports/exports to promotion and facilitation of exports/imports, keeping in view the interests of the country.

This Directorate, with headquarters at New Delhi, is responsible for implementing the Foreign Trade Policy with the main objective of promoting India's exports. The DGFT also issues licenses to exporters and monitors their corresponding obligations through a network of 38 regional offices and an extension counter in Indore.

All regional offices provide facilitation to exporters in regard to developments in international trade, i.e. WTO agreements, rules of origin and anti-dumping issues etc. to help exporters in their import and export decisions in an internationally dynamic environment.

Directorate General of Supplies and Disposal (DGS&D) with headquarters at New Delhi was closed on October 31, 2017. It functioned as the executive arm of the supply division of the Department of Commerce for conclusion of rate contracts for common user items, procurement of stores, consultancy etc. The functions of DGS&D were carried out through its functional wings and supporting service wings. The functional wings included the supply wing and the quality assurance wing. The supporting services wings included administration, vigilance, complaints and public relations, planning and co-ordination, internal work study, management information services, litigation etc.

The supply wing had commodity-wise purchase directorates such as information technology, electrical stores, mechanical engineering, automobiles, steel and cement, structural engineering, hardware, workshop and machine tools, wool, leather, paper and paper products, oil and chemicals. DGS&D has been transformed to a digital e-commerce portal for procurement and selling of goods and services, namely Government e Marketplace (GeM).

2.3.2 Directorate General of Trade Remedies (DGTR): DGTR (earlier Directorate General of Anti-Dumping and Allied Duties [DGAD]) was constituted in May 2018 as an integrated single window agency for providing comprehensive and swift trade defence mechanism in India. DGTR deals with anti-dumping, CVD and safeguard measures. It also provides trade defence support to the domestic industry and exporters in dealing with increasing instances of trade remedy investigations instituted against them by other countries. DGTR provides a level playing field to the domestic industry against the adverse impact of unfair trade practices like dumping and actionable subsidies from any exporting country, by using trade remedial methods under the relevant framework of WTO, Customs Tariff Act and Rules and other relevant laws and international agreements.

Between 1992 and 2013, DGAD initiated anti-dumping investigations into 295 cases. The countries prominently figuring in anti-dumping investigations were China, European Union, Taiwan, Korea, Japan, USA, Singapore, and Russia.

2.4 Subordinate Offices of the Department of Commerce

These are as follows:

2.4.1 Directorate General of Commercial Intelligence and Statistics (DGCI&S): DGCI&S is the premier organization of Government of India for collection, compilation and dissemination of India's trade statistics and commercial information. This Directorate, with its office located in Kolkata, is headed by the Director General. It is entrusted with the work of collecting, compiling and publishing/disseminating trade statistics and various types of commercial information required by the policy makers, researchers, importers, exporters, traders as well as overseas buyers.

2.4.2 Offices of Development Commissioner of Special Economic Zones (SEZs): The main objectives of the SEZ Scheme are generation of additional economic activity, promotion of exports of goods and services, promotion of investment from domestic and foreign sources, creation of employment opportunities along with the development of infrastructure facilities. All laws of India are applicable in SEZs unless specifically exempted as per the SEZ Act/ Rules. Each Zone is headed by a Development Commissioner and is administered as per the SEZ Act, 2005 and SEZ Rules, 2006. Units may be set up in the SEZ for manufacturing, trading or for service activity. The units in the SEZ have to be net foreign exchange earners but they are generally not subjected to any pre-determined value addition or minimum export performance requirements. Sales in the Domestic Tariff Area from the SEZ units are treated as if the goods are being imported and are subject to payment of applicable customs duties.

2.4.3 Pay and Accounts Office (Supply): The payment and accounting of Supply Division, including those of DGS&D, are performed by the Office of Chief Controller of Accounts (Supply Division) under the Departmentalized Accounting System.

Payment to suppliers for Rate Contract purchases has since been decentralized from January 1, 2014 with a provision of making of payment directly by indentors, i.e. order placing authority through their concerned Pay & Accounts Offices, instead of CCA (Supply) through its headquarters in New Delhi and regional offices situated in Kolkata, Mumbai and Chennai.

2.4.4 Pay and Accounts Office (Commerce and Textiles): Pay and Accounts Office, common to both the Department of Commerce and the Ministry of Textiles, is responsible for payment of claims, accounting of transactions and other related matters through the 4 Departmental Pay and Accounts Offices in Delhi, 2 in Mumbai, 2 in Kolkata and 2 in Chennai. These Departmental Pay and Accounts Offices are controlled by Principal Accounts Office in Delhi with Chief Controller of Accounts (CCA) as the Head of Department of Accounts Wing.

2.5 Autonomous Bodies under Department of Commerce

2.5.1 Commodity Boards: There are 5 statutory Commodity Boards under the Department of Commerce.

1. Tea Board.
2. Coffee Board.
3. Rubber Board.
4. Spices Board.
5. Tobacco Board.

These Boards are responsible for production, development and export of tea, coffee, rubber, spices and tobacco.

2.5.2 Marine Products Export Development Authority, Cochin: The Authority was set up as a Statutory Body in 1972 under an Act of Parliament. The Authority, with its headquarters in Kochi and field offices in all the Maritime States of India, is headed by a Chairman. The Authority is responsible for development of the marine industry with special focus on marine exports. It has Trade Promotion Offices in Tokyo (Japan) and New York (US).

2.5.3 Agricultural and Processed Food Products Export Development Authority (APEDA): APEDA was established by the Government of India under the Agricultural and Processed Food Products Export Development Authority Act passed by the Parliament in December 1985. The Act came into effect from February 13, 1986 by a notification issued in the Gazette of India. The Authority replaced the Processed Food Export Promotion Council (PFEPC).

It is entrusted with the task of promoting agricultural exports, including the export of processed foods in value added form. APEDA has also been entrusted with monitoring of export of 14 agricultural and processed food product groups listed in the Schedule to the APEDA Act. It is actively engaged in the development of markets besides upgradation of infrastructure and quality to promote the export of agro-products. In its endeavour to promote agro-products, APEDA provides financial assistance to the registered exporters under its schemes for: (a) market development, (b) infrastructure development, (c) quality development, (d) research and development and (e) transport assistance.

During 2009-10, APEDA was empowered by an Act of Parliament to enforce the Intellectual Property Right (IPR) of Geographical Indications (GI) for Basmati Rice.

2.5.4 Export Inspection Council (EIC), New Delhi: EIC was set up as a Statutory Body on January 1, 1964 under Section 3 of the Export (Quality Control and Inspection) Act, 1963 to ensure sound development of export trade of India through quality control and inspection and for matters connected therewith. It is an advisory body to the Central Government, with its office located in New Delhi and is headed by a Chairman. It is responsible for the enforcement of quality control and compulsory pre-shipment inspection of various commodities meant for export and notified by the Government under the Export (Quality Control and Inspection) Act, 1963.

EIC is assisted in its functions by the Export Inspection Agencies (EIAs), which are field organizations located in Chennai, Delhi, Kochi, Kolkata and Mumbai and have modern and accredited laboratories with the required logistic support for quality certification activities. These Agencies have a network of 36 sub-offices and laboratories located at different ports and major industrial centres to back up the pre-shipment inspection and certification activities.

2.5.5 Indian Institute of Foreign Trade (IIFT), New Delhi: IIFT is an autonomous body under the Ministry of Commerce and Industry to help professionalize the country's foreign trade management and increase exports by developing human resources, generating, analyzing and disseminating data and conducting research.

IIFT was registered in May 1963 under the Societies Registration Act, 1860. It was established by the Government of India with the objective to strengthen the country's external trade sector through development of human resources and by generating, analyzing and disseminating data, conducting research and providing consultancy services. Since then, it has been the pioneer in imparting training in foreign trade management in the country, besides undertaking research and consultancy in various areas of international business. It is because of its all round achievements that it was awarded the status of Deemed University in May 2002 by University Grants Commission (UGC) and accredited in May 2005 as A grade institution by National Assessment and Accreditation Council (NAAC).

To commensurate its achievement and contribution towards development of knowledge and growth of international trade, IIFT celebrated its Golden Jubilee on May 2, 2013.

IIFT has emerged as a major centre of international business by aligning its teaching, research and training capabilities with its core vision over the years and by constantly striving to create academic excellence through its five academic divisions, namely Graduate Studies Division (GSD), Research Division (RD), Management Development Programmes (MDPs) Division, International Collaboration and Capacity Development (ICCD) Division and International Project Division (IPD). Each division caters to competency development in a specific area and contributes to its overall growth.

2.5.6 Indian Institute of Packaging (IIP), Mumbai: It is an autonomous body set up by the Department of Commerce, Government of India in 1966 in partnership with the leading Indian packaging and allied industries. It is a society registered in Mumbai and works under the administrative control of the Department of Commerce.

IIP has the objective of promoting exports by helping innovate in design and development of packaging and also upgrading the packaging standards at the national level. It endeavours to achieve this by organizing educational courses and skill development programmes in packaging for the benefit of students and in-service packaging professionals, testing and certification of packaging, and provision of consultancy services to industry. It has created research and model infrastructural facilities at its location for training, design and development in packaging.

2.5.7 Indian Institute of Plantations Management (IIPM): Realizing the potentialities and needs of modernization of the plantation sector through management education and training, Ministry of Commerce and Industry, Government of India constituted a core group in 1990 to set up a strategic institution of management education in the plantation sector. Accordingly a blue-print for IIPM, Bangalore was prepared. This blue-print envisaged it as a centre of excellence, to act as a think tank and an intellectual resource base for the plantation sector. It also envisaged it as an exclusive sectoral school of management based on a new model intensive institute-industry interaction. After the acceptance of the blueprint by the Government, a steering committee of the Ministry of Commerce provided the initial thrust for setting up IIPM. In November 1993, it was registered as an autonomous educational institution of higher learning, under the Karnataka Society Registration Act. It is jointly sponsored by the plantation sector and the Commodity Boards, viz. Coffee Board, Tea Board, Rubber Board, Spices Board and Plantation Associations.

IIPM is actively supported by the industry through its uniquely designed Faculty Finance Support Scheme. Commodity Boards and several leading corporates have instituted chairs at the Institute. Currently, the chairs have been instituted by Tata Tea Limited, Goodricke Group Limited, WIlliamson Magor Group and Tata Coffee Limited. In return, IIPM provides intellectual support to the industry through its research, brainstorming workshops and seminars etc.

2.6 Public Sector Undertakings

2.6.1 The State Trading Corporation of India Limited (STC): STC was set up on May 18, 1956 primarily with a view to undertake trade with East European countries and to supplement the efforts of private trade and industry in promoting exports from the country. Since then, STC has played an important role in country's economy. It has arranged imports of essential items of mass consumption (such as wheat, pulses, sugar, edible oils, etc.) into India and contributed significantly in developing exports of a large number of items from India. The core strength of STC lies in handling exports/imports of bulk agro commodities. Over the years, STC has also diversified into exports of steel, iron ore, molasses and imports of bullion, hydrocarbons, minerals, metals, fertilizers, petro-chemicals etc. This has helped STC to achieve high level of performance in recent years. STC is today able to structure and execute trade deals of any magnitude, as per the specific requirement of its customers.

STC has 11 branch offices in India, the major ones being in Mumbai, Kolkata, Chennai, Ahmedabad, Bengaluru and Jalandhar.

2.6.2 Metals and Minerals Trading Corporation of India (MMTC): MMTC was created in 1963 as an independent entity on separation from State Trading Corporation of India primarily to deal in exports of minerals and ores and imports of non-ferrous metals. In 1970, MMTC took over imports of fertilizer raw materials and finished fertilizers. Over the years imports and exports of various other items like steel, diamonds, bullion, agro, hydrocarbon, have been added to the portfolio of the company.

MMTC has been following the mantra of strategic diversification for progress with much success, exploiting opportunities to expand base and open up new business prospects. It endeavours constantly to explore emerging opportunities by synergizing and blending them with its own core competencies, thereby creating new epicentres of growth and expanding its role as a trade organizer and facilitator. The company has participated in various value-multiplier initiatives to enhance its future sustainability through the joint venture (JV) and public-private-partnership (PPP) routes. MMTC has grown over the years to become one of the largest trading organizations in India.

To expand and give impetus to growing trade between India and Africa, MMTC opened an office in Johannesburg, South Africa in January 2011.

2.6.3 PEC Limited: PEC Ltd. (formerly The Project and Equipment Corporation of India Ltd.) was carved out of the STC in 1971-72 to take over the canalized business of STC's railway equipment division, to diversify into turn-key projects especially outside India and to aid and assist in promotion of exports of Indian engineering equipment. With effect from May 23, 1990, PEC Ltd. became a subsidiary of the then newly-formed holding company, Bharat Business International Ltd. Thereafter, from March 27, 1991, PEC Ltd. became an independent company directly owned by Government of India. The main functions of PEC Ltd. include exports of projects, engineering equipment and manufactured goods, defence equipment and stores, imports of industrial raw materials, bullion and agro commodities, consolidation of existing lines of business and simultaneously developing new products and new markets.

Over the years, business of PEC Ltd. has diversified with industrial raw materials, commodities and bullion, constituting major part of its turnover and profit.

2.6.4 Export Credit Guarantee Corporation of India Limited (ECGC): It was established in 1957 as the Export Risk Insurance Corporation of India. Keeping in view the wider role played by the Corporation, the name was changed to Export Credit Guarantee Corporation of India (ECGC). ECGC is the premier organization in the country which offers credit risk insurance cover to exporters, banks etc. Its primary objective is to promote country's exports by covering the risk of export on credit. It provides: (a) a range of insurance covers to Indian exporters against the risk of non-realization of export proceeds due to commercial or political causes and (b) different types of guarantees to banks and other financial institutions to enable them to extend credit facilities to exporters on liberal basis.

2.6.5 India Trade Promotion Organization (ITPO): The Trade Fair Authority of India (TFAI) and the Trade Development Authority (TDA) were merged together in 1992, and the new organization was renamed as India Trade Promotion Organisation (ITPO). ITPO is the premier trade promotion agency of India and provides a broad spectrum of services to trade and industry and acts as a catalyst for growth of India's trade.

With its headquarters at Pragati Maidan, New Delhi and regional offices in Bangalore, Chennai, Kolkata and Mumbai, ITPO ensures representative participation of trade and industry from different regions of the country in its events in India and abroad.

ITPO is a venue for exhibitions and conventions at its ground in Pragati Maidan in New Delhi. ITPO holds the India International Trade Fair (IITF) since 1980 every year. It is a premier international trade fair and has evolved as a major event for business community. Some of the exhibition buildings were demolished in April 2017 for re-development and after completion Pragati Maidan will be the biggest exhibition centre in Delhi.

The Department of Industrial Policy and Promotion of the Ministry of Commerce and Industry is developing India International Convention and Expo Centre as a world class facility over an area of 221.37 acres in Sector 25 of Dwarka, New Delhi at an estimated cost of ₹ 25,703 crore. The foundation stone for the Project was laid by Prime Minister Shri Narendra Modi on September 20, 2018. Phase-I has been completed and Phase-II will be completed by December 2024.

2.7 Advisory Bodies

2.7.1 Board of Trade (BOT): BOT was set up on May 5, 1989 with a view to provide an effective mechanism to maintain continuous dialogue with trade and industry in respect of major developments in the field of international trade. It, *inter alia*, advises the Government on policy measures connected with the Foreign Trade Policy in order to achieve the objectives of boosting India's exports.

Terms of reference BOT are as under:

1. To advise the Government on policy measures for preparation and implementation of both short and long-term plans for increasing exports in the light of emerging

national and international economic scenario.

2. To review export performance of various sectors, identify constraints and suggest industry-specific measures to optimize export earnings.
3. To examine the existing institutional framework for imports and exports and suggest practical measures for further streamlining to achieve the desired objectives.
4. To review the policy instruments and procedures for imports and exports and suggest steps to rationalize and channelize such schemes for optimum use.

2.7.2 Inter-State Trade Council: This Council was set up on June 24, 2005 with a view to serve as a mechanism for institutionalized dialogue between the Union and the States in matters relating to trade facilitation and to create a framework for making States partners in India's export effort. The Council is represented by Chief Ministers of the States, Lieutenant. Governors/Administrators of the Union Territories, Secretaries of various Ministries of the Government of India and Chairman, Railway Board. It also co-opts the Chairman-cum-Managing Director of Export Credit Guarantee Corporation, Managing Director of EXIM Bank, Deputy Governor of Reserve Bank of India, Chairman of Agricultural and Processed Food Products Export Development Authority, Chairman of Marine Products Export Development Authority and presidents of CII, FICCI, FIEO, ASSOCHAM and Export Promotion Council for EOUs/SEZs.

2.8 Other Organisations

2.8.1 Federation of Indian Export Organisations (FIEO): FIEO, set up in 1965 under the Societies Registrations Act of 1860, is the apex body of various export promotion organizations and institutions. With major regional offices in Delhi, Mumbai, Chennai and Kolkata, the main objective of FIEO is to render an integrated package of services to various organizations connected with export promotion. It provides the content, direction and thrust to

India's global export efforts. It also functions as a primary servicing agency to provide integrated assistance to its members which comprise professional exporting firms holding recognition status granted by the Government, consultancy firms and service providers. It organizes seminars and arranges participation of its members in various exhibitions in India and abroad.

2.8.2 Indian Council of Arbitration (ICA), New Delhi: ICA, India's premier arbitral institution, is a society registered under the Societies Registration Act, 1860. With its head office in New Delhi and 8 branches with a pan-India network, it operates on no-profit basis. Established in 1965, it promotes and administers the use of Alternative Dispute Resolution mechanisms in commercial disputes, thereby encouraging greater domestic and international commerce. The main objective of ICA is to provide arbitration facilities for amicable and quick settlement of commercial disputes with a view to maintaining the smooth flow of trade, particularly export trade on a sustained and enduring basis.

2.8.3 Indian Diamond Institute (IDI), Surat: IDI was established as a Society in 1978 with the objective of enhancing the quality, design and global competitiveness of the Indian jewellery. Located in Surat, IDI is sponsored by the Department of Commerce, Ministry of Commerce and Industry, Government of India and patronized by the Gems and Jewellery Export Promotion Council (GJEPC). IDI conducts various diploma and other courses related to diamond trade and industry. The 3 year diploma course in diamond, gem and jewellery design and manufacture conducted by IDI has been accredited by All India Council for Technical Education (AICTE). IDI also has certification services for diamonds, coloured stones and gold jewellery.

2.8.4 Footwear Design and Development Institute (FDDI): FDDI was established in the year 1986 as a society under the Societies Registration Act, 1860 with the objective to train the professional manpower for footwear industry. It is an

ISO:9001 and ISO:14001 certified Institute, which conducts wide range of long-term and short-term programmes in the area of retail management, fashion, footwear merchandising, marketing, creative design and leather goods and accessories design etc. It provides one stop solution to the footwear industry and is internationally acclaimed as one of the premier institutes in the area of footwear design, technology and management.

2.8.5 National Centre for Trade Information (NCTI): National Centre for Trade Information (NCTI): It was incorporated on March 31, 1995 as a company under Section 25 of the Companies Act, 1956. The company started functioning w.e.f. March 1996. It has a board of directors for administration of its affairs, which includes representatives from Ministry of Commerce and Industry, National Informatics Centre (NIC), Indian Institute of Foreign Trade (IIFT), and Directorate General of Commercial Intelligence and Statistics (DGCI&S). Other representatives are from India Trade Promotion Organisation (ITPO) and other export promotion councils.

2.8.6 Price Stabilization Fund (PSF) Trust: PSF Scheme was launched by Government of India in April 2003 against the backdrop of decline in international and domestic prices of tea, coffee, rubber and tobacco, causing distress to primary growers. The growers of these commodities were particularly affected due to substantial reduction in unit value realization for these crops, at times falling below their cost of production. The objective of the scheme was to safeguard the interests of the growers of these commodities and provide financial relief when prices fall below a specified level. The scheme was operationalized through the Price Stabilization Fund Trust. The PSF Scheme period ended on September 30, 2013 and a revised scheme proposal—modified Price Stabilization Fund Trust (2013)—is under consideration of the Government.

2.8.7 GS1-India: GS1-India is a not-for-profit standards body promoted by the Ministry of Commerce and Industry, Government of India and Indian industry to spread awareness and provide guidance on adoption of global standards in supply chain management by Indian industry for the benefit of consumers, industry, Government etc.

GS-1 India is the only organisation in India authorised to issue company prefix numbers for use in barcodes etc. for unique, unambiguous and universal identification of products, cartons, containers etc. GS-1 standards find wide application in supply chains across sectors for unique-yet-universal product, consignment and entity identification, EDI (Electronic Data Interchange), product data synchronisation etc. GS-1 standards are the de facto global standards in identification of consumer products in retail. GS1-India is an affiliate of GS-1 Global Office, twin headquartered in Brussels (Belgium) and New Jersey (US), which oversee operations of a network of over 100 GS-1 organisations across the world.

2.8.8 India Brand Equity Foundation (IBEF): It is a trust established by the Department of Commerce, Ministry of Commerce and Industry, Government of India in 2003 with the objective of promoting and creating international awareness of the Made in India label in markets overseas and to facilitate dissemination of knowledge of Indian products and services. Towards this objective, IBEF works closely with stakeholders across government and industry.

3

Post-Independence Trade Policy

Over the last 72 years, India's foreign trade has undergone a complete change in terms of composition and direction. The exports cover a wide range of traditional and non-traditional items while imports mainly consist of capital goods, petroleum products, raw materials, and chemicals to meet the ever-increasing needs of a developing and diversifying economy. This chapter describes and examines changes in the pattern of India's foreign trade since Independence in 1947, with focus on developments since 1991.

3.1 Partition and the Aftermath

The partition of the country in 1947 cut across its economic and cultural unity and the growth of centuries of common life to which all the communities had contributed. Whatever might have been the political justification of partition, its economic consequences were disastrous. Regions which had functioned for centuries on a complementary basis were suddenly cut asunder. Economically, India and Pakistan had each, points of advantages and disadvantages. In general, it may be said that while India was much stronger at that time in industrial production and mineral resources, Pakistan had some advantage in agricultural resources, especially foodstuffs. In fact, the complementary character of their economies was even deeper than is indicated by this generalisation.

Partition affected most the exports of jute, cotton, and hides. In the new set-up, large scale imports of these were essential for some of the largest established industries in India. However, the commodities that could be exported to Pakistan in exchange were mainly processed materials like cotton textiles, sugar, and matches which, until Partition, were receiving some protection against foreign competition in the areas which in the new set up went to Pakistan. Partition therefore not only resulted in increased reliance on imported raw materials but made more difficult the problem of export promotion.

3.2 Depletion of Sterling Balances

The main feature in the external financial position of the country soon after Independence was the sharp decline in the sterling balances held by the Reserve Bank of India, the growing difficulty in the financing of imports from the hard currency areas and the emergence of Pakistan as a foreign country for currency purposes with the separation of its currency from that of India.

The rapid depletion of the sterling balances after Independence caused some anxiety to the Government of India. These balances represented the entire foreign exchange reserves of the country and it was of the utmost importance that they were not frittered away on the import of non-essential and luxury articles. The view of the Government of India was that these reserves should not be used to finance deficits in the balance of payments on what was called normal current account. The aim was to meet normal day-to-day requirements from abroad through the earnings of current exports and draw upon these accumulated reserves, broadly speaking, only for the purpose of purchasing capital goods, the import of which was necessary for developing the agricultural and industrial productivity of the country.

With this aim in view, the Government of India decided to follow a more restrictive import policy from the second half of the calendar year 1947. Broadly speaking, that policy consisted of dividing imports into three categories: free, restricted and prohibited. Imports of food, capital goods, the raw materials of industry and certain essential consumer goods were free and no exchange restrictions were placed upon their import. Consumer goods which were not absolutely essential were licensed on a quota basis, while others which in the context of the economy of

India were regarded as totally unessential and luxury imports were altogether prohibited. Together with the restrictions on imports, certain restrictions on remittances abroad, in particular on the transference of Indian capital were also introduced.

3.3 Empire Dollar Pool

India had always displayed an interest in the arrangement commonly known as the Empire Dollar Pool. The arrangement was that the countries of the sterling area hold all their foreign exchange reserves in sterling, selling currencies which they did not need to the Bank of England, and buying from the Bank of England currencies which were in short supply. As a consequence, there was always in the custody of the Bank of England, a pool of foreign exchange from which members of the sterling area could buy for sterling, the currencies which they needed. A more correct name for this arrangement was "the Sterling Area Pool of Foreign Exchange". It had come to be known as the Empire Dollar Pool only because the most important of the foreign exchanges in the pool was the United States dollar.

3.4 Devaluation of the Rupee in September 1949

The problem of holding the prices in check was one of the major preoccupations of Government in the years following Independence. The steps taken to remedy the situation included the devaluation of the rupee in September 1949. After this event, price cuts in certain essential commodities were made in an effort to counter the possible effects of devaluation, and this assisted in holding the price level for some time. In fact, the general price index fell by 12 points from 393.3 at the end of October 1949 to 381.3 at the end of December 1949. It did not, however, prove possible to check for long the upward pressure on prices generated by devaluation, and by June 1950 the gain secured during the closing months of the previous year had been lost, the index number standing at 395.6.

The outbreak of the Korean War gave a further impetus to

the rise in prices and by September the index number had risen to 412.5. This increase in prices was, however, not peculiar to India and to a very great extent it reflected the upward movement in prices in other countries which supplied important categories of our imports.

3.5 Korean War and the Export Boom

One result of the development in the international situation, following the outbreak of the Korean War, was to intensify the demand for some of the principal exports from India like jute goods, raw cotton, cotton waste and raw wool. The external prices of these commodities rose very steeply and in view of both the interests of the exchequer and the necessity for countering inflation, it was decided that this difference should be intercepted by Government through the enhancement or levy of export duties. Export duties on jute goods and raw cotton were accordingly enhanced while new duties were imposed on exports of cotton waste and wool. In the rapidly changing conditions, Government also considered it necessary to obtain from Parliament temporary powers to enhance, if necessary, existing export duties and to levy new duties. All these measures had a steadying effect on prices although it was not possible wholly to arrest an upward trend.

While the internal economic conditions were a matter of continuous concern for Government, the position with regard to the balance of payments was more heartening. An improvement in the balance of payments began with the devaluation of the rupee in September 1949 and this improvement was maintained, the process being assisted by the changes in the international situation following the outbreak of hostilities in Korea. Except for a short period during the second quarter of 1950, when a slight seasonal fall in exports and heavy payments for imports of raw cotton resulted in a small deficit, the overall position was favourable since the last quarter of 1949.

3.6 Trade Agreement with Pakistan, 1950

Following the non-devaluation of the Pakistan rupee, when other members of the sterling area devalued their currencies in September 1949, trade between the two countries had come to a virtual standstill. The effect of the non-devaluation of the Pakistan rupee was to cause an immediate increase in the price which importers in India had to pay for Pakistan goods, of which the most important single item was raw jute. A rise in the price of raw jute, at a time when the jute mills were faced with difficulties in maintaining their markets against the competition of substitutes, was a matter of great concern to India. If the prices in Pakistan had been allowed to fall to the appropriate levels under the normal action of the forces of supply and demand, it might have been possible for India to buy her raw jute and the continuity of purchase by India need not have been broken.

India's willingness to buy Pakistani goods, if they were available at reasonable prices, was amply demonstrated by the trade agreement which was signed in April 1950. Under it, Indian jute mills were to be supplied raw jute by Pakistan, to be paid for in Indian rupees at prices comparable to the price of Indian jute. These rupees were available to Pakistan for the purchase in India of certain specified commodities like jute manufactures, cotton textiles, cement, timber etc.

Under the stimulus of the devaluation of the rupee and the boom in prices which followed the outbreak of the Korean War, India accumulated a substantial surplus in its balance of payments during 1950-51 and in the early months of 1951-52. During this period, the country could not import as much as it wished owing to the difficulty of obtaining supplies from abroad. In consequence, the domestic stocks of essential supplies fell to a low level and it became essential to take measures to restore the stocks by reducing exports of cotton textiles, oil and oil seeds, and by stepping up imports of raw materials and essential consumer goods.

3.7 Devaluation of the Rupee in June 1966

A major task of policy in the 1960s was to conserve scarce foreign exchange resources and to secure progressive increases in export earnings. The budget for 1963-64 increased import and excise duties with a view to curtail the consumption of commodities which were chiefly imported. The increase in direct taxation was accompanied by concessions in respect of exports. The gold policy of the Government was also directed towards conservation of foreign exchange which financed the smuggling of gold and while some features of the Gold Control were eased to meet the transitional problem arising from the unemployment of goldsmiths, there was no slackening of efforts to discourage the use of gold in the country. These and other measures resulted in a degree of improvement in the balance of payments position in the 1960s.

In order to bring domestic prices in line with external prices, to restore and enhance the competitive power of exports, and to provide a solution to the country's trade and payments problems, the par value of the rupee was reduced by 36.5 percent on June 6, 1966, involving a rise of 57.5 percent in the price of foreign exchange in terms of Indian rupees. Along with devaluation, the existing special export promotion schemes providing import entitlements against exports and the scheme for tax credit certificates were abolished. Moreover, in order to protect the unit values of exports in terms of foreign exchange, export duties were levied on a number of commodities, mostly agricultural commodities and agriculture-based manufactures. A variety of additional measures were taken to promote exports.

A liberal import policy was announced for 59 priority industries, including a number of export-oriented industries. A new import replenishment scheme enabled registered exporters to obtain raw materials, components and spares against export of specified products. If was decided to provide cash assistance for exports of selected products with a good export potential. A scheme for the supply of steel at international prices to exporters of engineering goods was announced. Imports of some raw materials were placed under an Open General Licence.

On the side of imports, the principal policy measure taken with devaluation was the announcement of a liberal import policy for 59 priority industries under which arrangements were made to meet their requirements for raw materials, components and spares in full (initially for six months). The import policy for small-scale industrial units making the same products as the priority industries was also substantially liberalised.

3.8 Import Substitution: Cornerstone of Trade Policy

India adopted an inward-looking development strategy after independence wherein import substitution constituted a major element of both trade and industrial policies. The focus in the initial stages of planned development was on stimulating "home-grown" industrialisation, essentially based on the "infant industry argument", wherein production for domestic market was shielded behind high tariff walls and high effective protection. This strategy of import-substituting industrialisation created self-fulfilling biases against the export-producing sectors and as such, exports were relegated to the periphery as a "residual" sector. This policy not only underestimated the export possibilities but also the import intensity of the import substitution process itself.

Import substitution was the prime objective of India's trade policy till the mid-1970s. This policy was largely based on the Imports and Exports (Control) Act of 1947 and the Import Trade Control Order of 1955. Liberal incentives were granted to firms if they were undertaking production of an imported item that was not domestically produced.

The need to correct the "anti-export" bias was gradually recognised and, in the 1970s, several export promotion measures were put in place in the form of export incentives and export services to generate higher exports on a sustained basis. Protective quotas, however, remained more or less intact and domestic industry continued to be shielded from import competition. The policies relating to foreign trade became subject of intense discussions in the early 1980s with export competitiveness receiving maximum attention. It became increasingly clear that production for exports cannot be isolated from production for the home market and that trade policy would have to be integrated with the policy for domestic industrialisation. The licensing and highly regulated trade policy slowly started giving way to a more open regime from the early 1980s, gathering further momentum during the second half of the decade.

A three-year Export-Import Policy was introduced in 1985 to provide a definite focus to the trade sector. A major ingredient of this policy was the provision of easy access to essential capital goods, raw materials and components from abroad since these were viewed as a major incentive for exporters in undertaking technological upgradation for reducing costs and improving quality. Notwithstanding these measures, the trade regime in the 1980s continued to be characterised by the overwhelming presence of the licensing mechanism and a high level of tariffs isolating the economy from external competition, constrained further by restrictive industrial and foreign investment policies.

In short, prior to mid-1991, foreign trade of India suffered from strict bureaucratic and discretionary controls. Similarly, foreign exchange transactions were tightly controlled by the Government and the Reserve Bank of India. Beginning mid-1991, the Government of India introduced a series of reforms to liberalise and globalise the Indian economy. Reforms in the external sector of India are intended to integrate the Indian economy with the world economy. In this context, the Ninth Five Year Plan (1997-2002) observed, "The process of globalisation is a reality which cannot be denied and also should not be avoided. However, it needs to be managed so that we can derive the maximum advantage from world markets". [1]

3.9 Balance of Payments Crisis, 1991

Despite the robust export performance during the Seventh

Five Year Plan (1985-90) period, a number of medium-term factors such as the declining self-sufficiency in crude oil and petroleum products, the erosion of surpluses in the invisibles account, an unfavourable climate for external assistance, and the bunching of debt service obligations, continued to strain the external payments position, while the problem was exacerbated by a number of short-term factors.

The balance of payments situation became very difficult in 1991-92 despite the softening of oil prices in the world market. Hence, even with a substantial import compression, the pressures on the balance of payments persisted throughout the current financial year.

Accordingly, the Government attempted to mobilize support for the balance of payments from multilateral financial institutions—the International Monetary Fund, the World Bank and the Asian Development Bank—as well as from bilateral donors, for immediate relief.

Another important initiative taken by the Government to meet the urgent need for balance of payments financing was the announcement of two schemes designed to encourage the inflow of capital funds from abroad. The India Development Bond Scheme and the Immunity Scheme for repatriation of funds held abroad were introduced in October 1991.

3.10 East Asian Crisis

The East Asian crisis, which continued to deepen and spread in 1998, led to tremendous volatility and uncertainty in global financial markets, and to a restructuring-evaluation of emerging markets as investment destinations. The increased risk aversion of international capital had an impact on all emerging economies, including to some extent in India. In spite of a turbulent international environment, India's balance of payments remained moderately comfortable.

The trade deficit increased from 3.7 percent of GDP in 1996-97 to 3.9 percent in 1997-98, despite the sharp deceleration in import growth. This was attributable to deceleration in export growth, which continued for the third year in succession in 1998-99.

The weakness in export performance reflected various international and domestic factors.

3.11 Gender Sensitization of Trade Policy

United Nations Conference on Trade and Development (UNCTAD) organized an International Conference on Moving towards Gender Sensitization of Trade Policy in New Delhi from February 25 to 27, 2008.

The conference provided a forum for Indian and international trade and gender experts to discuss and raise awareness on trade performance and gender linkages in India and globally and propose actions and directions towards enhanced and more effective gender sensitisation of trade policy with particular reference to India and generally to developing countries.

Equitable distribution of gains from trade among thc genders is a development objective which needs to be addressed through trade policies and trade agreements. Women are significant stakeholders in the process of trade, growth and development. This must be recognized and harnessed by Government to make globalization more inclusive with pro-poor impact. Women's groups must be consulted to a greater extent and in a systematic and structured manner, in the formulation of trade policicies or negotiating positions, so as to integrate the gender dimension, he suggested.

Broadly, the Conference deliberations suggested a strong and direct relationship between trade performance, gender empowerment and development, explicit and specific attention to gender issues in policy and operational actions, as well as in attitudes, are key conditions for maximizing the gains for gender empowerment through trade and minimizing the costs that can arise. This is important because overall the situation in India and in many developing countries presently is that there is progress towards gender empowerment through trade.

Moreover, a gender-sensitive approach to trade must involve a vision of trade as an integral component of wider development efforts to eradicate poverty and promote inclusive, people-centred development.

3.12 Initiation of Reforms in the Foreign Trade Sector

The balance of payments position, which had reached a point of near collapse in June 1991, slowly stabilized during the course of 1991-92. Although new policies to deal with the situation were quickly formulated by the new Government and implemented within a few months, the external payments situation took time to stabilize primarily because it had been allowed to deteriorate to a state of near bankruptcy in June 1991. Foreign currency reserves had declined to US$ 1.1 billion despite heavy borrowing from the IMF in 1990-91 and a substantial part of this was held in illiquid deposits, which could not have been easily mobilised if needed.

The strategy for the management of the balance of payments outlined in the Budget for 1991-92, which was presented in July 1991, relied upon a combination of macro-economic stabilisation and structural reforms in industrial and trade policy. It was recognized that in the medium term, the solution to the balance of payments problem would have to come from a much stronger export performance, but in the short-run, the strategy had to be underpinned by mobilization of external financing from the multilateral agencies and from bilateral donors. Restoration of access to imports through liberalization had to depend initially upon additional financing since the export efforts would take time to show results. Since access to external commercial borrowing was constrained, the only other sources of funds were the bilateral and multilateral agencies. Visible support from the multilateral agencies was important for restoring international confidence.

Accordingly, the Government negotiated a standby arrangement with the IMF in October 1991 for US$ 2.3 billion over a 20-month period, a Structural Adjustment Loan with the

World Bank of US$ 500 million and a Hydrocarbon Sector Loan with the ADB for US$ 250 million.

With the assurance of external support through these efforts, there was a gradual stabilization of the balance of payments position in the course of 1991-92. Foreign exchange reserves were restored to more normal levels, increasing from US$ 1.1 billion in June 1991 to US$ 5.6 billion at the end of March 1992.

Import restrictions were gradually lifted in the course of 1991-92 as the balance of payments stabilized. By the end of 1991-92, the new Liberalized Exchange Rate Management System introduced in the Budget for 1992-93 eliminated import licensing in most capital goods, raw materials, intermediates and components and introduced a dual exchange rate system with one rate effectively floated in the market. The Budget for 1992-93 also reduced customs duties in line with declared Government policy in order to make the Indian economy more competitive and gradually exposing Indian industry to external competitive pressure. The trade and exchange policy regime for 1992-93 was therefore characterised by major progress in eliminating unnecessary administrative and discretionary controls over foreign trade, which were contributing to making the economy uncompetitive.

Reform of trade and exchange rate policy was a critical element in structural reform and a great deal was done in this area. The exchange rate adjustments in July 1991, and the trade policy announced subsequently, considerably reduced the reliance upon licensing control of imports and created a more favourable exchange rate for exports, especially when account was taken of the premium on Eximscrips. The introduction of the Liberalized Exchange Rate Management System (LERMS) moved further in the direction of eliminating licensing control and allowing the exchange rate to reflect the scarcity of foreign exchange. The system had worked fairly well during 1992-93.

The dual exchange rate under which exporters got a weighted average of the official rate and the market rate, was criticised as amounting to a tax on exporters. The reduction in tariffs in the previous two Budgets, and the change in the exchange rate over this period had obviously been of considerable benefits to exporters. This improvement was moderated, but by no means eliminated, by the implicit tax in the present dual rate. The Government indicated that this was a transitional arrangement. It was the intention of the Government to move towards full convertibility on the current account, including unification of the exchange rate, over a period of two to three years.

Although licensing restrictions were greatly reduced, they were not entirely eliminated. There was need to review the remaining licensing restrictions and remove as many items as possible from licensing and canalisation. These restrictions were out of place in the existing situation of the balance of payments position.

The policy of progressively lowering customs tariffs was an essential element of any strategy for making the Indian economy internationally competitive. Government took important steps in this direction; but Indian tariff rates, with a maximum tariff of 110 percent (except for selected consumer items, which were much higher) remained much above the levels prevailing in other countries. The Chelliah Committee had made recommendations for a bold reduction in tariffs to be phased over the next four years. It was necessary to implement these recommendations in an appropriate manner.

Parallel with these developments, the rigours of exchange control were mitigated. The Foreign Exchange Regulation Act was amended by an Ordinance in January 1993 to remove a number of constraints on foreign exchange dealings and various restrictions on firms with foreign equity holdings.

Major steps were taken in 1993 to promote exports. The Export-Import Policy announced on April 1, 1993 amended the existing policy to provide a greater thrust to exports from agriculture and labour-intensive sectors in which the country had a strong comparative advantage. The negative list for exports was significantly pruned. A new Export Promotion Capital Goods Scheme permitting import of capital goods at a concessional 15 percent duty rate was introduced for the services sector.

Export-oriented units (EOUs) and export processing zones (EPZs) in agriculture and allied sectors were allowed to sell up to 50 percent of their total output in the domestic market. Fiscal and financial policy was also deployed to support the export effort. Import duties were reduced on capital goods used in textiles, readymade garments, leather, marine products, gems and jewellery, food processing and horticulture. The pre-shipment credit facility in foreign currency was greatly liberalised, thus, providing Indian exporters credit at internationally competitive rates of interest. A number of steps were taken to strengthen facilities and incentives available for export through export processing zones, 100 percent export oriented units and electronics hardware technology parks.

Endnote

1. Government of India, Planning Commission, *Ninth Five Year Plan* (1997-2002), Volume I, p. 5.

4

Export-Import (EXIM) Policy: 1992-97, 1997-2002 and 2002-07

India's foreign trade is regulated by the Foreign Trade (Development and Regulation) Act, 1992 which replaced the Import and Export (Control) Act, 1947. The Act of 1992 empowers the Central Government to formulate and announce from time to time the export and import policy and to amend it in like manner.

Prior to mid-1991, foreign trade of India suffered from strict bureaucratic and discretionary controls. However, the new Government which took over at the Centre in June 1991 soon realised that India's foreign trade policy must respond to the changes (liberalisation and openness) sweeping across the world. To reduce controls, simplify procedures and to create a congenial environment for trade, the Government made a Statement on Trade Policy in Parliament on August 13, 1991, ushering a new era in the foreign trade policy of India. Instead of controls and regulations, the focus shifted to promotion and development of foreign trade.

Before 1985-86, an annual export-import policy was announced by the Government of India at the beginning of the financial year. In 1985-86, a three year Export-Import (EXIM) Policy was announced for the period April 1985 through March 1988, providing a reasonable degree of stability to the policy framework. On its expiry, a new EXIM Policy for three years 1988-91 was announced in March 1988 which laid greater emphasis on promotion of exports.

EXIM Policies 1992-97, 1997-2002 and 2002-07 coincided with the periods of Eighth Five Year Plan, Ninth Five Year Plan and Tenth Five Year Plan respectively. It is noteworthy that EXIM Policy 2002-07 was incorporated in the

Foreign Trade Policy 2004-09 announced by the Government on August 31, 2004.

Objectives, strategies and measures contained in the EXIM Policies 1992-97, 1997-2002 and 2002-07 are presented below.

4.1 EXIM Policy, 1992-97

On March 31, 1992, the Government announced the Export and Import Policy for a period of five years (April 1, 1992 to March 31, 1997), coinciding with the period of Eighth Five Year Plan. The Chief Controller of Imports and Exports was re-designated as Director General of Foreign Trade (DGFT). The office of the DGFT is responsible for formulation and execution of foreign trade policy, including licensing.

EXIM Policy, 1992-97 made a conscious effort to dismantle various protectionist and regulatory policies and accelerate India's transition towards a globally oriented economy. The export-import policy was further liberalised by the Government on March 31, 1993. Substantial concessions were announced to boost agricultural exports. The Government also announced a Centrally- sponsored scheme to set up industrial parks in different states.

4.2 EXIM Policy, 1997-2002

The Export and Import Policy, 1997-2002 (coinciding with the period of Ninth Five Year Plan) sought to consolidate the gains of the previous policy and further carry forward the process of liberalisation by deregulating and simplifying procedures and removing quantitative restrictions in a phased manner. It set an ambitious target of attaining an export level of US$ 90-100 billion by the year 2002 and achieving 1 percent share in world trade.

4.2.1 Objectives: The principal objectives of the policy were the following.

1. To accelerate the country's transition to a globally-oriented vibrant economy to derive maximum benefits

from expanding global market opportunities.

2. To stimulate sustained economic growth by providing access to essential raw materials, intermediates, components, consumables and capital goods required for augmenting production.
3. To enhance the technological strength and efficiency of Indian agriculture, industry and services, thereby improving their competitive strength while generating new employment opportunities, and encourage the attainment of internationally accepted standards of quality.
4. To provide consumers with good quality products at reasonable prices.

4.2.2 Salient Features: Following were the salient features of the Policy.

1. Exports and imports shall be free, except to the extent they are regulated by the provisions of this Policy.
2. The Central Government may, in public interest, regulate the import or export of goods by means of a Negative List of Imports or a Negative List of Exports, as the case may be.
3. The Negative Lists may consist of goods, the import or export of which is prohibited, restricted through licensing, or canalised.
4. Prohibited items in the Negative List of Imports shall not be imported and prohibited items in the Negative List of Exports shall not be exported.
5. Any goods, the export or import of which is restricted through licensing, may be exported or imported only in accordance with a licence issued in this behalf.
6. Any goods, the import or export of which is canalised, may be imported or exported by the canalising agency specified in the Negative List.
7. No export or import shall be made by any person without an Importer-Exporter Code (IEC) number unless specifically exempted.

4.2.3 Modified EXIM Policy, April 1998: The new

Government at the Centre, which assumed office in March 1998, announced its Export and Import Policy for the year 1998-99 on April 13, 1998. As part of the annual export-import policy modification, the Government freed from import restrictions a large number of consumer goods and liberalised all major export promotion schemes. This new dose of liberalisation of the trade regime by the new Government was necessitated by the commitments made by India at the World Trade Organization (WTO). The timing of the import policy liberalisation coincided with the scheduled review of India's trade policy by WTO on April 16 and 17, 1998. Apart from the general global pressure on India to remove restrictions on imports, the US had filed a complaint with the WTO against India's import regime. The following were the main provisions of the modified Export-Import Policy unveiled by the Commerce Minister on April 13, 1998.

1. 340 more items were shifted from the restricted list to Open General Licence (OGL). Thus, out of the total number of 10, 202 items covered under the export-import policy, only 2,200 remained on the restricted list.
2. The revised policy set an export growth target of 20 percent for the year 1998-99 which in other words required total exports of the order of US$ 41.4 billion during 1998-99.
3. Zero-duty Export Promotion Capital Goods (EPCG) scheme was extended to all software exporters by lowering the threshold limit of importable capital goods from ₹ 20 crore to ₹ 10 lakh. The lowering of threshold limit was expected to help software companies to proliferate throughout the length and breadth of the country. In other words, they could import any capital goods without paying any import duty and in return sign an export obligation of 5 times the value of capital goods on net foreign exchange earnings basis for a period of six years. In the case of garments, agriculture, food processing, gems and jewellery, electronics, leather, sports goods and toys, the

minimum limit was lowered to ₹ 1 crore.

4. In a bid to prevent cheap imports being dumped at unreasonable prices, the Government set up an anti-dumping cell called Directorate General (DG) of Anti-Dumping and Allied Duties. The DG would be responsible for investigation into alleged cases of dumping as well as subsidised cases. The DG would also recommend anti-dumping duties where it is found that dumped imports are causing harms to the domestic industry. Where harm is caused to domestic industry by subsidising exports by the exporting country, then the DG would have the jurisdiction to investigate all such cases and recommend possible imposition of countervailing duties. The DG would also advise the industry groups and consumer fora on how to go about collecting information and procedures involved in making out a case for anti-dumping duties.
5. Other provisions included:

- delegation of powers to regional licensing offices,
- doing away with the minimum value addition of 33 percent under advance licensing scheme,
- simplified procedures for clubbing of advance licence schemes, and
- private bonded warehouses to be set up to import, stock and sell even negative list items.

4.2.4 EXIM Policy, 1999-2000: In its effort to further dismantle the import control regime and hasten the integration of the Indian economy with the world economy, the Government announced a revised export-import policy on March 31, 1999 which came into force on April 1, 1999.

The new export-import policy freed import of 894 items of consumer goods, agricultural products and textiles from licensing requirements. In other words, a number of consumer items could now be imported license-free subject only to the payment of import duty. Physical controls on imports were removed and the only control over imports was fiscal in nature, i.e. adjusting import duty to regulate imports. These adjustments were to be made within the upper limits prescribed by WTO. Moreover, another 414 items were removed from the *restricted list*, allowing these to be imported against special import licenses. India's international commitments require it to remove licensing curbs on imports by the year 2003.

4.2.5 EXIM Policy, 2000-01: The Union Commerce and Industry Minister announced on March 31, 2000 the new Export-Import Policy of the Government of India for the year 2000-2001. The export-import policy, envisaging a 20 percent export growth in dollar terms in 2000-2001, brought about a major rationalisation in export promotion schemes and launched a series of sector-specific initiatives.

A. Export Promotion: In a major initiative to boost exports, the Government announced the following measures:

(a) Special Economic Zones (SEZs): On the pattern of the Chinese model, the Government announced the setting up of two SEZs, at Positra in Gujarat and Nangunery in Tamil Nadu. Industrial units located in SEZs will be exempted from a plethora of rules and regulations governing exports and imports. The entire production will have to be exported from these zones. Sales from domestic tariff area (DTA) can be done only on full payment of customs duty. Several export processing zones (EPZs) will shortly be converted into SEZs. The EPZs located in Kandla, Vizag and Kochi will be converted into SEZs immediately. It was further announced that 100 percent foreign direct investment (FDI) would be allowed in all products in SEZs.

SEZs would be treated as if they are outside the customs territory of the country. The units would be able to import capital goods and raw materials duty free. The movement of goods to and from SEZs would be unrestricted.

It is noteworthy that SEZs have played a crucial role in boosting China's exports and presently the country derives 40 percent of its exports from such zones. However, Chinese SEZs are based on contract labour system (hire and fire policy). The Commerce Minister while announcing the EXIM Policy categorically ruled out any changes in labour laws. Moreover, there is no system of reservation of items for small-scale industries in China. It is unclear if the Government of India would allow the production of reserved items for small industries in the SEZs. Still further, there are various infrastructural bottlenecks like power shortage, lack of transport facilities and of course procedural delays. Hence, the success of SEZs in India is a moot question.

(b) Sector-specific Packages: The Export-Import Policy 2000-2001 announced sector-specific packages for seven core areas to boost exports, viz. gems and jewellery, pharmaceuticals, agrochemicals, biotechnology, silk, leather and garments.

For the gems and jewellery exporters, the Government announced a diamond-dollar account (DDA) scheme. Under the scheme, export proceeds can be retained in a dollar account and the exporters can use funds in this account for import of rough diamonds.

For agro-chemicals, biotechnology and pharma units (considered as knowledge-intensive), the Government has allowed duty-free import of laboratory equipment, chemicals and reagents up to 1 percent of the FOB value of exports. Similarly, the Government increased duty-free import of trimmings, embellishments and other items from 2 to 3 percent of total export values.

B. Import Liberalisation: The Export-Import Policy 2000-01 lifted quantitative restrictions on 714 commonly used items (agricultural products and consumer durables) which can now be freely imported. Thus, commodities like meat, milk powder, coffee, tea, fish, pickles, cigars and cigarettes, televisions, radios, tape recorders, footwear and umbrellas can be imported freely from April 1, 2000. However, most of these items will attract peak rate of basic import duty.

The lifting of licensing and quota restrictions on 714 import items was in line with India's WTO obligations. The Government promised to abolish licensing and quota curbs on the remaining

715 items (such as liquor, cars etc.) in April 2001.

Many critics of the new policy fear that removal of licensing and quota restrictions would lead to surge in imports of these items, hurting the domestic industry. However, it is noteworthy that import restrictions are being phased out since 1996 but no extraordinary growth has occurred in the import of freed items. The Commerce Minister maintained that anti-dumping and anti-subsidy tariffs and other safeguards would be used if there is a sudden surge in imports, causing serious injury to the domestic industry.

4.2.6 EXIM Policy, 2001-02: The Union Commerce and Industry Minister unveiled on March 31, 2001, the Export-Import Policy for the year 2001-02.

A. Removal of Quantitative Restrictions: The process of removal of import restrictions, which began in 1991, was completed in a phased manner by the Export-Import Policy 2001-02 with the removal of restrictions on the remaining 715 items. This was in tune with the commitments made to the WTO. Out of these 715 items, 342 were textile products, 147 were agricultural products and 226 were other manufactured products.

However, import of agricultural products like wheat, rice, maize, copra and coconut oil was placed in the category of State Trading. The nominated State Trading Enterprise will conduct the import of these commodities solely as per commercial considerations. Similarly, import of petroleum products including petrol, diesel and ATF was placed in the category of State Trading. In all, 27 out of 715 items taken off the quantitative restrictions list were put under the State Trading category.

The Minister was confident that the Indian market will not be swamped by imported brands of commonly used articles. To prevent dumping, Government will take recourse to anti-dumping duties and other non-tariff barriers. Arrangements have been made to track, collate and analyse data on 300 sensitive items which mainly comprise farm goods and items produced by small-scale sector.

B. Agricultural Export Zones: With a view to boost agricultural exports and provide remunerative returns to the farming community, the Export-Import Policy proposed the setting up of agricultural export zones. Three such zones are proposed to be set up in Himachal Pradesh, Jammu and Kashmir (to promote export of apples) and Maharashtra. Government will make efforts to provide improved access to the produce/products of the agriculture and allied sectors in the international market. State Governments have been asked to identify product specific agricultural export zones for development for export of specific products from a geographically contiguous area.

4.3 EXIM Policy, 2002-07

EXIM policy 2002-07 was unveiled on March 31, 2002. The policy entailed several institutional, infrastructural and fiscal measures intended to promote exports which are conducive to the economic development of the country. It emphasised export market diversification with special focus on unexploited regions like sub-Saharan Africa and the CIS. It also stressed on a farm-to-port approach for exports of agricultural products, special thrust on cottage sectors and handicrafts and beefed up Assistance to States for Infrastructural Development for Exports (ASIDE).

The following were the salient features of the Policy.

4.3.1 Special Economic Zones (SEZs): Offshore banking units (OBUs) were permitted in SEZs. Units in SEZ were permitted to undertake hedging of commodity price risks, provided such transactions are undertaken by the units on stand-alone basis. This will impart security to the returns of the unit.

It has also been decided to permit external commercial borrowings (ECBs) for a tenure of less than three years in SEZs. The detailed guidelines will be worked out by RBI. This will provide opportunities for accessing working capital loan for these units at internationally competitive rates.

4.3.2 Employment Generation: In an effort to generate additional employment, the following announcements were made pertaining to agricultural and small industry sectors.

1. Export restrictions like registration and packaging requirement were removed forthwith on butter, wheat and wheat products, coarse grains, groundnut oil and cashew to Russia. Quantitative and packaging restrictions on wheat and its products, butter, pulses, grain and flour of barley, maize, bajra, ragi and jowar had already been removed on March 5, 2002.
2. Restrictions on export of all cultivated varieties of seed, except jute and onion, were removed.
3. To promote export of agriculture and agriculture-based products, 20 agriculture export zones were notified.
4. In order to promote diversification of agriculture, transport subsidy shall be available for export of fruits, vegetables, floriculture, poultry and dairy products.
5. 3 percent special DEPB rate was announced for primary and processed foods exported in retail packaging of 1 kilogram or less.
6. An amount of ₹ 5 crore under Market Access Initiative (MAI) was earmarked for promoting cottage sector exports coming under the KVIC.
7. The units in the handicrafts sector can also access funds from MAI scheme for development of website for visual exhibition of their product.
8. Under the Export Promotion Capital Goods (EPCG) scheme, these units will not be required to maintain average level of exports, while calculating the export obligation.
9. These units shall be entitled to the benefit of Export House Status on achieving lower average export performance of ₹ 5 crore as against ₹ 15 crore for others.
10. The units in handicraft sector shall be entitled to duty free imports of an enlarged list of items as embellishments up to 3 percent of FOB value of their exports.

With a view to encouraging further development of centres of economic and export excellence such as Tirupur for hosiery, woollen blanket in Panipat, woollen knitwear in Ludhiana, following benefits shall be available to small scale sector:

1. Common service providers in these areas shall be entitled for facility of EPCG scheme.
2. The recognised associations of units in these areas will be able to access the funds under the Market Access Initiative scheme for creating focused technological services and marketing abroad.
3. Such areas will receive priority for assistance for identified critical infrastructure gaps from the scheme on Central Assistance to States.
4. Entitlement for Export House Status at ₹ 5 crore instead of ₹ 15 crore for others.

4.3.3 Technology Upgradation: Electronic Hardware Technology Park (EHTP) scheme was modified to enable the sector to face the zero duty regime under ITA (Information Technology Agreement)-1. The units shall be entitled to following facility.

1. Net foreign exchange as a percentage of exports (NFEP) positive in 5 years.
2. No other export obligation for units in EHTP.
3. Supplies of ITA-I items having zero duty in the domestic market to be eligible for counting of export obligation.

4.3.4 Growth-oriented: The status holders shall be eligible for the following new/special facilities.

1. Licence/certificate/permissions and customs clearances for both imports and exports on self-declaration basis.
2. Fixation of input-output norms on priority.
3. Priority finance for medium and long-term capital requirement as per conditions notified by RBI.
4. Exemption from compulsory negotiation of documents through banks. The remittances, however, would continue to be received through banking channels.
5. 100 percent retention of foreign exchange in exchange

earners' foreign currency (EEFC) account.

6. Enhancement in normal repatriation period from 180 days to 360 days.

4.3.5 EXIM Policy, 2003-04: It had the following provisions.

1. The policy provided a massive thrust to export of services by introducing duty free import facility for the service sector units having a minimum foreign exchange earning of ₹ 10 lakh.
2. Encouragement of corporate sector with proven credential to sponsor agri-export zones for boosting farm exports.
3. EPCG scheme made more flexible and attractive so that even the small scale sector could set up and expand its manufacturing base for exports.
4. Fixing of input-output norms for status holders on priority basis within a period of 60 days and permission to status holders in Software Technology Parks of India (STPI) for free movement of professional equipments.
5. Simplification and codification of rules, regulations and procedures applicable to SEZ and EOU units by putting all these rules and regulations in one place, thus greatly facilitating both potential investors and existing units.
6. To increase the overall competitiveness of export clusters, a scheme for upgradation of infrastructure in existing clusters/industrial locations would be implemented.
7. Extension of Duty Free Replenishment Certificate (DFRC) scheme to deemed exports and reduction in its value addition norms from 33 percent to 25 percent.

4.3.6 Mini EXIM Policy, January 2004: Preceding the dissolution of the 13th Lok Sabha on February 6, 2004, the Government of India announced a mini EXIM policy on January 28, 2004. It included facilitation and simplification measures to sustain the momentum of export growth. Specifically, it was aimed at providing boost to exports of gems and jewellery, encouraging tourism (domestic and foreign) and making energy generation cheaper. Highlights of the new policy were:

1. Free import of gold and silver for export purposes permitted. In other words, gold and silver can now be imported without paying any commission to channelling agents. (In 1997, the Government authorized three canalizing agencies, viz. MMTC, STC and HHEC, and eight banks to import gold and silver for sale in the domestic market). Likewise, import of rough, uncut and semi-polished diamonds will not be valued for export obligations. Quantitative restrictions on gold and silver imports have also been lifted. Government also announced the introduction of a gold card for creditworthy exporters to make available cheaper foreign currency debt on easier terms.
2. Duty-free import facility available to star hotels extended to heritage, one and two-star hotels and stand-alone restaurants. All these hotels have been allowed duty-free import equivalent to 5 percent of their export earnings in three preceding years.
3. Restrictions on import of electrical energy lifted.
4. Online licenses and electronic fund transfer facility for exporters. These measures are expected to reduce transaction cost for exporters, and make export administration transparent.

5

Foreign Trade Policy (FTP): 2004-09, 2009-14 and 2015-20

The long-term vision of the Government is to make India a major player in world trade by 2020, and assume a role of leadership in the international trade organisations commensurate with India's growing economic and demographic profile. In consonance with its vision of ensuring sustained accelerated growth of exports and making India a major player of world trade, the government announces a Foreign Trade Policy (FTP) every five years. FTP is annually reviewed to incorporate changes necessary to take care of emerging economic scenarios both domestically and globally. The Department of Commerce, Ministry of Commerce and Industry, Government of India, formulates, implements and monitors FTP which provides the basic framework of a medium-term strategy to be followed for promoting exports and trade.

On August 31, 2004, Government of India announced a Foreign Trade Policy for 2004-09 (September 1, 2004 to March 31, 2009) to provide a stable policy framework.

India's FTP 2009-14 was announced on August 27, 2009 in the backdrop of economic turmoil of 2008. FTP, 2009-14 set out a goal of doubling India's exports of goods and services by 2014, with the long-term objective of doubling India's share in global trade by the end of 2020 through appropriate policy support.

On April 1, 2015, Government announced the Foreign Trade Policy for the period 2015-20

The underlying philosophy of India's FTP is based on seven broad principles:

1. Give a focused thrust to exports of employment intensive industries.

2. Encourage domestic manufacturing for inputs to export industry and reduce the dependence on imports.
3. Promote technological up-gradation of exports to retain a competitive edge in global markets.
4. Persist with a strong market diversification strategy to hedge the risks against global uncertainty.
5. Encourage exports from the North-Eastern Region given its special place in India's economy.
6. Provide incentives for manufacturing of green goods recognising the imperative of building capacities for environmental sustainability.
7. Endeavour to reduce transaction cost through procedural simplification and reduction of human interface.

The trade performance of a country is so closely and inextricably linked with its overall economic performance that trade policy cannot be treated as a simple matter of manoeuvring the export or import of a product. Foreign trade policy has a direct connect with domestic economic policies. Exports constitute the last segment of a long sectoral value chains. A foreign trade policy that addresses only the front-end of exports without recognising the characteristics of the back-end is incomplete and, likely to be unworkable.

Objectives, strategies and measures contained in the various Foreign Trade Policies are presented below.

5.1 Foreign Trade Policy (FTP), 2004-09

In a radical move, the Government of India announced, on August 31, 2004, a new Foreign Trade Policy for the period 2004-09, replacing the hitherto nomenclature of EXIM Policy by Foreign Trade Policy (FTP). A vigorous export-led growth strategy of doubling India's share in global merchandise trade in the next five years, with a focus on the sectors having prospects for export expansion and potential for employment generation, constituted the main plank of the Policy. These measures were expected to enhance international competitiveness and aid in further increasing the acceptability of Indian exports.

5.1.1 Objectives and Strategy: The new Foreign Trade Policy (FTP) took an integrated view of the overall development of India's foreign trade and essentially provided a roadmap for the development of this sector. It was built around two major objectives of doubling India's share of global merchandise trade by 2009 and using trade policy as an effective instrument of economic growth with a thrust on employment generation. Key strategies to achieve these objectives, *inter alia*, included the following:

1. Unshackling of controls and creating an atmosphere of trust and transparency.
2. Simplifying procedures and bringing down transaction costs.
3. Neutralizing incidence of all levies on inputs used in export products.
4. Facilitating development of India as a global hub for manufacturing, trading and services.
5. Identifying and nurturing special focus areas to generate additional employment opportunities, particularly in semi-urban and rural areas.
6. Facilitating technological and infrastructural upgradation of the Indian economy, especially through import of capital goods and equipment.
7. Avoiding inverted duty structure and ensuring that domestic sectors were not disadvantaged in trade agreements.
8. Upgrading the infrastructure network related to the entire foreign trade chain to international standards.
9. Revitalizing the Board of Trade by redefining its role and inducting into it experts on trade policy; and activating Indian Embassies as key players in the export strategy.

5.2 Foreign Trade Policy (FTP), 2009-14

India's FTP, 2009-14 was announced on August 27, 2009 in the backdrop of economic turmoil of 2008. FTP, 2009-14 set out a goal of doubling India's exports of goods and services

by 2014, with the long-term objective of doubling India's share in global trade by the end of 2020 through appropriate policy support. The short-term objective was to arrest and reverse the trend of decline in exports and provide additional support to those sectors that had been badly hit by the crises.

To attain the policy objectives, FTP, 2009-14 used a mix of policy instruments including fiscal incentives, institutional changes, procedural rationalization, obtaining enhanced market access across the world, and diversification of export markets. Improvement in infrastructure related to exports, reducing transaction costs, and providing full refund of all indirect taxes and levies, were the three crucial pillars of the policy.

FTP, 2009-14, incorporating provisions relating to export and import of goods and services, came into force with effect from August 27, 2009 and remained in force up to March 31, 2014.

5.2.1 Special Focus Areas: With a view to continuously increasing percentage share of global trade and expanding employment opportunities, certain special focus initiatives were been identified/continued for market diversification, technological upgradation, support to status holders, agriculture, handlooms, handicraft, gems and jewellery, leather, marine, electronics and IT hardware manufacturing industries, green products, exports of products from North-East, sports goods and toys sectors. Government made concerted efforts to promote exports in these sectors by specific sectoral strategies that were notified from time to time.

5.2.2 Market Diversification: Weaker demand in developed economies, triggered by falling asset prices and increased economic uncertainty had pulled down the growth of India's exports to developed countries. There were no clear signals as to when the markets in developed countries would revive. To insulate Indian exports from the decline in demand from developed countries, the focus in FTP, 2009-14 was on diversification of Indian exports to other markets, especially those located in Latin America, Africa, parts of Asia and Oceania. To achieve diversification of Indian exports, following initiatives were taken.

1. 26 new countries were included within the ambit of Focus Market Scheme.
2. Incentives provided under Focus Market Scheme were increased from 2.5 percent to 3.0 percent.
3. There was a significant increase in the outlay under Market Linked Focus Product Scheme by inclusion of more markets and products. This ensured support for exports to all countries in Africa and Latin America.

5.2.3 Technological Upgradation: To usher in the next phase of export growth, India needs to move up in the value chain of export goods. This objective was sought to be achieved by encouraging technological upgradation of export sector. A number of initiatives were taken in this Policy to focus on technological upgradation.

5.2.4 Support to Status Holders: To incentivise and encourage the status holders, as well as to encourage technological upgradation of export production, additional duty credit scrip @ 1 percent of the FOB of past export was granted for specified product groups including leather, specific sub sectors in engineering, textiles, plastics, handicrafts and jute. This duty credit scrip could be used for import of capital goods by these status holders. The imported capital goods were subjected to actual user condition.

5.3 Foreign Trade Policy (FTP), 2015-20

Foreign Trade Policy (FTP) for the period 2015-20 announced by the Government on April 1, 2015 explains the vision, goals and objectives of India's foreign trade. It describes the market and product strategy envisaged and the measures required not just for export promotion but also for the enhancement of the entire trade ecosystem. FTP, 2015-20 has the following components.

5.3.1 Vision, Mission and Objectives: The vision is to make India a significant participant in world trade by the year 2020 and to enable the country to assume a position of leadership in the international trade discourse. Government aims to increase India's exports of merchandise and services from US$ 465.9 billion in 2013-14 to approximately US$ 900 billion by 2019-20 and to raise India's share in world exports from 2 percent to 3.5 percent.

FTP, 2015-20 provides a stable and sustainable policy environment for foreign trade in merchandise and services. It details procedures and incentives for exports and imports with other initiatives—such as *Make in India, Digital India* and *Skills India*—to create an *Export Promotion Mission.* It seeks to promote diversification of India's export basket by helping various sectors of the Indian economy to gain global competitiveness. It envisages an architecture for India's global trade engagement with a view to expanding its markets and better integrating with major regions, thereby increasing the demand for India's products. It provides a mechanism for regular appraisal in order to rationalise imports and reduce the trade imbalance.

5.3.2 Whole-of-Government Approach: Foreign trade today plays a significant part in India's economy, so much so that it deserves a special focus and dedicated attention as a key constituent of India's economic policies. Foreign trade policy can neither be formulated nor implemented by any one department in isolation. Going forward, a *whole-of-government* approach is required. A major path-breaking initiative of FTP, 2015-20, which can have far-reaching benefits if properly executed, is to mainstream State and Union Territory (UT) Governments and various Departments and Ministries of the Government of India in the conduct of international trade.

5.3.3 Addressing In-house Challenges: The state of the external environment undoubtedly will be crucial and new features of the global trading landscape such as mega regional agreements and global value chains will profoundly affect India's trade. The biggest challenge, however, is to address constraints within the country such as infrastructure bottlenecks, high transaction costs, complex procedures, constraints in manufacturing and inadequate diversification of exports of services. FTP, 2015-20 has identified winners and potential winners from amongst industrial and agricultural products in order to make the export promotion schemes more focused and effective. At the same time, an institutional mechanism for continuous import appraisal has been put in place to ensure coordinated and rational import policies in various sectors.

5.3.4 Aligning FTP with WTO: The need to ensure that the FTP is aligned with both India's interests in the negotiations, as well its obligations and commitments under various WTO Agreements, has been an important consideration in framing FTP, 2015-20. In the ongoing Doha Round of trade negotiations, India will continue to work towards fulfilling its objectives and to work with like-minded members to remove any asymmetries in the multilateral trade rules which place a developing country at a disadvantage, such as the rules relating to public stockholding for food security purposes.

5.3.5 Market Strategy: India's future bilateral/regional trade engagements will be with regions and countries that are not only promising markets but also major suppliers of critical inputs and have complementarities with the Indian economy. The focus of India's future trade relationship with its traditional markets in the developed world would be on exporting products with a higher value addition, supplying high quality inputs for the manufacturing sector in these markets and optimizing applied customs duties on inputs for India's manufacturing sector.

5.3.6 Product Strategy: The focus will be on promoting exports of high value products with a strong domestic manufacturing base, including engineering goods, electronics, drugs and pharmaceuticals. The challenges posed to the pharmaceuticals sector by non-tariff barriers (NTBs) in Japan and regulatory hurdles in China have to be addressed. A track and trace policy for all exports of medicinal products will be effective from April 1, 2015. A composite programme for promotion of healthcare products and services will be conducted in various regions to showcase and market India's unique strengths.

Other sectors which require special attention, in light of India's strengths and their contribution to employment generation, are leather, textiles, gems and jewellery and the sectors based on natural resources, which include agriculture, plantation crops, marine products and iron ore exports. Revitalizing plantations, enabling a less controlled regime for agriculture and aiming at greater value addition and processing would help to increase the value of exports from these sectors. Export strategies for processed agricultural exports and organic product exports will shortly be ready. The North-Eastern States are a special focus area for organic product exports. A number of steps to address the challenges faced by the plantations sector are on the anvil.

Further, Government aims to encourage and promote hi-tech products and, as a first step, certain products have been identified for a special focus for the duration of the policy. The potential of the micro, small and medium enterprises (MSMEs) sector, the problems it faces and its requirements have been kept in view while framing the FTP, 2015-20.

5.3.7 Brand Building: Government is committed to transforming India into a manufacturing and exporting hub. This is possible only if India's products are of world class standard. A roadmap has been developed on measures required to protect consumers, raise the quality of the merchandise produced and enhance India's capacity to export to even the most discerning markets. A long-term branding strategy has been conceptualised to enable India to hold its own in a highly competitive global environment and to ensure that Brand India becomes synonymous with high quality. Further, a programme to promote the branding and commercialisation of products registered as Geographical Indications and to promote their exports will be initiated within one year of this policy coming into force.

5.3.8 Anchoring Trade Policy in the Domestic Policy Framework: There is a symbiotic relationship between the FTP and the Government's Make in India initiative. The Make in India initiative aims to achieve global recognition for the Indian economy, promote the country as an investment destination, spur manufacturing and promote employment. It encompasses initiatives for skill development to ensure the availability of skilled manpower for manufacturing, to improve the ease of doing business through initiatives such as self-certification of documents and innovative revenue models. It also envisages the development of infrastructure including i-ways besides highways, ports, optical fibre networks, gas grids and water grids.

There is a clear recognition within Government that exports should not merely be a function of marketable surplus but should reflect a genuine enhancement of economic capacity and development. Through its foreign trade policy, government envisages as follows:

1. Employment creation in both manufacturing and services through the generation of foreign trade opportunities.
2. Zero defect products with a focus on quality and standards.
3. A stable agricultural trade policy encouraging the import of raw material where required and export of processed products.
4. A focus on higher value addition and technology infusion.
5. Investment in agriculture overseas to produce raw material for the Indian industry.
6. Lower tariffs on inputs and raw materials.
7. Development of trade infrastructure and provision of production and export incentives.

5.3.9 Focus of the FTP: FTP, 2015-20 is primarily focused on accelerating exports. This is sought to be implemented through various schemes intended to exempt and remit indirect taxes on inputs physically incorporated in the export product, import capital goods at concessional duty, stimulate services exports and focus on specific markets and products. The Policy attempts to dovetail these schemes with the specific market access openings that India has achieved through negotiations with its trading partners for various bilateral and regional trading arrangements.

In order to make these schemes more focused and effective, an exercise was undertaken to identify products that are winners and potential winners for export purposes, based on their price competitiveness, the CAGR of India's exports and world imports and revealed comparative advantage (RCA) and areas of strength, both now and in the future. These have been identified separately from amongst industrial and agricultural products.

Further, in order to realise the objective of exporting more value-added goods, technology intensive sectors have also been identified for hand-holding by the Government in the next five years.

5.3.10 Import Appraisal: Striking a balance between meeting the needs of a growing economy and the promotion of domestic industry is a continuous challenge for policy makers. An institutional mechanism for continuous import appraisal would provide valuable inputs for economic policy in general and trade policy in particular. A mechanism has been put in place by the Department of Commerce for quarterly appraisal of imports. The 21 stakeholder Ministries/Departments which have been identified have been advised to probe into the need for importing various commodities and the feasibility of producing them in a cost effective way. The objective is to develop an ecosystem conducive to formulating coordinated and rational import policies in various sectors.

5.3.11 Measures Needed to Achieve Objectives: In order to achieve these objectives, the way forward requires measures to:

1. Help improve India's export competitiveness and deepen engagements with new markets.
2. Operationalise institutional mechanisms in existing bilateral and regional trade agreements.

3. Deepen and widen the export basket.
4. Reduce transaction costs.
5. Make efforts to reduce the cost of export credit.
6. Help improve infrastructure, e.g. ports, laboratories and common facility centres.
7. Promote product standards, packaging and branding of Indian products.
8. Rationalise tax incidence by introducing goods and services tax (GST).
9. Help improve manufacturing by mainstreaming exports.
10. Incentivise potential winners for promising markets.
11. Promote and diversify exports of services.
12. Mainstream States and Ministries in India's export strategy.

These measures cut across several Departments and Ministries of the Government of India and also State Governments. The success of trade policy is critically dependent on the coordinated efforts of the Government of India as a whole as well as State governments.

6

Composition and Destination of Exports

Exports have acquired added significance in the wake of liberalisation wave sweeping across the world. The trend towards market economy in almost all the countries of the world has increased the role of exports in developmental efforts. Exports have become an important indicator of a country's economic performance.

6.1 Post-Independence Export Performance at a Glance

At least for two decades after Independence, i.e. from 1947 to closing years of 1960s, India's export growth was very low bordering stagnation. To a certain extent this was attributable to the lack of coherent domestic policies since even in traditional exports India's share in world exports declined. However, this was not a period of rapid growth in exports from developing countries and India's export growth rate was comparable to that of other developing countries. The real difference between India and other countries was evident after 1965 when, right up to 1971 the country could not profit from the boom in world trade.

Hence, a series of measures were initiated with the object of stepping up exports. It is possible that but for these efforts exports during this period might have been lower. The measures in question were fairly widely conceived and included organisational changes, increased facilities and incentives and diversification of trade. These included the following:

1. Export Promotion Councils were set up for cotton textiles, silk and rayon, engineering goods, chemicals, tobacco, spices, cashew, leather, plastics, sports goods and mica.
2. Establishment of the Export Risks Insurance Corporation.

3. Assignment of the duties of Export Promotion Councils to Commodity Boards for tea, coffee and coir.
4. Increased facilities for publicity, fairs, exhibitions etc.
5. Removal of export controls and quota restrictions.
6. Abolition of most export duties.
7. Refund of excise duties.
8. Special import licences for raw materials for exports.
9. Priorities for transport facilities.
10. Development of trading relations with USSR and countries in Eastern Europe.

Export growth after 1971 was much more impressive and India's exports grew nearly as rapidly as those of the countries classified as fast growing exporters of manufactures. One further feature of the growth in exports over this later period was the diversification in terms of commodities and foreign markets.

Export performance during the Ninth Five Year Plan (1997-2002) was less than satisfactory and this fact was well-documented in the Tenth Five Year Plan (2002-07) which observed, "The Ninth Plan had envisaged a growth of 11.8 percent per annum in exports, against which the actual growth was 5.6 percent (in dollar terms) during the Ninth Plan period. Even this unsatisfactory performance was accompanied by high volatility. Exports had recorded a negative growth of 3.9 percent during 1998-99. The year 2000-01 witnessed a high growth of 19.6 percent but declined sharply to 0.05 percent in 2001-02. The Ninth Plan had also envisaged that the export-GDP ratio would be 10.4 percent, but the likely outcome would be lower, at around 9 percent". [1]

The drastic reduction in growth rate of exports during 2001-02 was primarily due to structural constraints operating on the demand as well as on the supply side. The recessionary tendencies across the world affected the demand for India's exports as well. Such slow-down and contraction of world trade also resulted in emergence of protectionist policies by developed countries in some sectors in the form of barriers of technical, environmental and social standards, affecting market access and disrupting exports from India.

Furthermore, movements of the exchange rate also affected export performance. Major supply constraints that continue to hamper India's exports include infrastructural constraints, high transaction costs, reservation for small scale industries, labour inflexibility, constraints in attracting FDI in exports sector and maintenance of product quality.

Till 1991, India occupied a very small space on the global trade canvas. As liberalization of the external sector started in that year, exports began to grow remarkably. Presently, foreign trade plays a significant part in the Indian economy reflecting its increasing globalisation. At the same time, the growing merchandise trade deficit, resulting in a persistently high current account deficit, has set alarm bells ringing. Trade policy, therefore, aims at promoting exports along with making imports more focussed and rational.

Both external and domestic factors have posed a challenge to export growth such as the global trade slowdown from 2008-09 onwards, exchange rate fluctuations and non-tariff barriers imposed by India's trading partners and loss of competitiveness in many product areas. The inherent limitations of manufacturing in India, the lack of diversity and focused efforts on services exports, the under achievement of the potential of SEZs, high transaction costs, high cost of trade finance and infrastructural bottlenecks are the domestic challenges to be overcome. The heavy dependence on imports of essential commodities including crude oil, gas, coal, pulses, edible oils, fertilizers and electronics has kept India's trade deficit at a high level.

6.2 Composition of Exports

The pattern of export trade during 1950-60 was marked by two main trends: (a) exports did not improve on the whole for commodities which were directly or largely based on agricultural production such as tea, cotton textiles, jute manufactures, hides and skins, spices and tobacco and (b) significant increases were achieved in the exports of new manufactures and of products like iron ore, but these were not sufficient to offset the decline in the traditional exports.

Although the opening up of the Indian economy since the early 1990s provided an impetus for higher growth for most export commodities, some products gained more than the others. Export products like iron and steel, petroleum products and pharmaceuticals gained both in terms of growth rate as well as share in the export basket. On the other hand, there were products such as, cotton, leather, tea and readymade garments that lost out in the export market in terms of export share.

The surge in exports relative to imports has provided a strong stimulus to domestic industrial growth. While software exports are a well-known success story, India is now an important venue for many tasks in services such as financial accounting, call centres, processing insurance claims, and medical transcription. The future potential for growth in these areas appears to be considerable.

The changing structure of India's exports throws some interesting light on both the demand pattern and supply factors that are increasingly influencing India's exports and the manner in which its production structures, institutions and policies are responding to it. The nature and extent of the export performance, however, need to be assessed not only by India's share in global exports but also with regard to its structural pattern, compositional shift and competitiveness.

India's merchandise exports are predominated by the manufacturing sector which accounted for more than three-fourth of its total exports during the 1990s. There has, however, been considerable re-orientation of relative importance of products within the manufacturing sector. The main drivers within the manufactured product groups were chemicals and allied products, engineering goods, ready-made garments, textile yarn, fabrics and gems and jewellery.

The products wherein India has the maximum presence in international market in terms of export share are spices, marine products, precious and semi-precious stones, textiles. Recent trends, however, indicate that the commodity structure of India's exports has slowly begun to shift towards higher technology intensive manufactures.

Contrary to India's experience, the improvement in technology intensity of exports has been almost dramatic for most of the East Asian countries and to some extent also for China. The areas in which Southeast Asian countries achieved their highest export growth during the 1980s were typically labour intensive, relatively low technology products such as textiles, clothing, toys, shoes and sports goods. Subsequently, during the 1990s, they graduated up to somewhat higher technology consumer goods and then to even higher technology and capital intensive sectors such as capital goods and petrochemicals.

Composition of India's exports in 2018-19 is shown in Table 6.1. Presently, India's export drivers include project exports, IT sector, gems and jewellery, textiles, engineering goods, chemicals, and ores and minerals. Services exports have imparted the fastest thrust to overall export growth.

Table 6.1: Commodity Composition of India's Exports: 2018-19

(Descending order)

S. No.	Commodity	US$ million
1.	Engineering goods	83,621
2.	Petroleum products	46,544
3.	Gems and jewellery	40,251
4.	Organic and inorganic chemicals	19,223
5.	Drugs and pharmaceuticals	19,146
6.	Ready made garments of all textiles	16,138
7.	Cotton yarn/fabrics/made-ups, handloom	11,254
8.	Electronic goods	8,829
9.	Plastics and linoleum	8,607
10.	Rice	7,753
11.	Marine products	6,802

contd...

12.	Leather and leather products	5,140
13.	Man-made yarn/fabrics/made-ups	4,980
14.	Meat, dairy and poultry products	4,364
15.	Mica, coal and other ores, and minerals	4,253
16.	Spices	3,322
17.	Ceramic products and glassware	2,649
18.	Fruits and vegetables	2,538
19.	Handicrafts excluding handmade carpets	1,838
20.	Cereal preparations	1,554
21.	Oil meals	1,511
22.	Carpets	1,482
23.	Iron ore	1,318
24.	Oilseeds	1,157
25.	Tobacco	981
26.	Tea	831
27.	Coffee	822
28.	Cashew	654
29.	Other cereals	349
30.	Jute manufactures, floor coverings	325
31.	Other commodities	21,867
32	Total exports	3,30,070

Note: Total may differ due to rounding off of individual items.
Source: Reserve Bank of India, *Handbook of Statistics on Indian Economy, 2018-19*, Table 120; data rearranged.

Micro, small and medium enterprises (MSMEs) contribute about 45 percent of the manufacturing output, over 40 percent of the total exports of the country, and around 8 percent of the country's GDP. They contribute significantly to employment generation and the development of rural areas. MSMEs sector is one of the key drivers of India's transition from an agrarian economy to an industrialized one, through its contribution to improving entrepreneurial skills and economic empowerment. MSMEs feed local consumer markets and international value chains. The sector currently produces more than 6,000 quality products, ranging from handloom sarees, carpets, soaps and pickles, to auto and machine parts targeting both domestic and international markets.

6.3 Destination of Exports

Prior to Independence, India's trade relations were confined mainly to Britain and other Commonwealth countries. Over the last 72 years, significant changes have taken place in India's direction of exports and sources of imports. USA, Germany, Japan, Russia and Middle East countries have emerged major trade partners of India.

A market diversification strategy based on the changing dynamics of growth in the world economy is necessary to ensure sustained growth of exports.

The core of the market strategy must therefore be as under:

1. Retain presence and market share in "old developed country markets".
2. Move up the value chain in providing products in these old developed country markets.
3. Open up new vistas, both in terms of markets and new products in these new markets.

India would have to focus on markets in Asia (including ASEAN), Africa and Latin America. It must establish new beachheads and strengthen presence in newly opened up markets. At the same time, it should aim to deepen engagement in the older markets, by increasing volumes, targeting increased shares for exports in the import baskets of large importers of export products, and diversifying the product basket of exports.

Since the initiation of economic reforms, India's outward orientation has increased considerably. The destination pattern of Indian exports has remarkably changed in the sense that the importance of developing countries as an export market has considerably increased. There are, however, concerns that the country has not been able to fully utilise its potential in international trade. In contrast to the dramatic changes in exports of East Asia, India's experience has seemingly fallen short of expectation. India's share in global trade has not increased as impressively and the commodity structure of India's exports remained almost unchanged until the mid-1990s.

Table 6.2 shows the relative significance of various country groups and countries in India's exports for the year 2018-19.

Table 6.2: Destination of India's Exports: 2018-19

Country Group	**US$ million**
I. OECD countries, of which	1,28,175
A. European Union, of which	57,203
a. France	5,232
b. Germany	8,902
c. UK	9,309
B. North America, of which	55,258
a. Canada	2,851
b. USA	52,407
C. Asia and Oceania, of which	8,762
a. Australia	3,520
b. Japan	4,862
D. Other OECD countries, of which	6,952
a. Switzerland	1,187
II. OPEC countries, of which	48,780
a. Iran	3,511
b. Iraq	7,789
c. Kuwait	1,334
d. Saudi Arabia	5,562
e. UAE	30,126
III. Eastern Europe, of which	3,504
a. Russia	2,390
IV. Developing countries, of which	1,46,517
A. Asia, of which	1,08,508
a. China	16,749
b. South Korea	4,705
c. Singapore	11,571
B. Africa	24,166
C. Latin America	13,843
V. Others	188
VI. Unspecified	2,905
TOTAL EXPORTS	3,30,070

Source: Reserve Bank of India, *Handbook of Statistics on Indian Economy, 2018-19*, Table 134.

Department of Commerce, Ministry of Commerce and Industry, Government of India has identified 15 strategic overseas locations where the Trade Promotion Organisations (TPOs) are proposed to be created. India has great potential to generate greater volumes of export with these countries. TPOs are proposed at the following locations:

1. Astana (Kazakhstan).
2. Beijing (China).
3. Cape Town (South Africa).
4. Dubai (UAE).
5. Frankfurt (Germany).
6. Ho Chi Minh City (Vietnam).
7. Jakarta (Indonesia).
8. Lima (Peru).
9. London (U.K.).
10. Melbourne (Australia).
11. Mexico City (Mexico).
12. Moscow (Russia).
13. New York (USA).
14. Sao Paulo (Brazil).
15. Tokyo (Japan).

Endnote

1. Government of India, Planning Commission, *Tenth Five Year Plan* (2002-07), Volume I, p. 101.

7

Product-wise Export Strategy

In order to raise India's share in world exports from 2 percent to 3.5 percent, it is essential to focus efforts on those sectors where India already has strengths as well as those which have untapped potential. A Strategy Paper [1] prepared by the Department of Commerce in 2010 identified such sectors, based on various considerations which continue to be relevant today.

Promoting the growth of exports from high value creating and employment-generating sectors with a strong domestic manufacturing base, would be the lynchpin of India's overall export growth strategy.

Further, based on domestic manufacturing capabilities and potential demand, exports of drugs and pharmaceuticals, chemicals and electronics (all high value products reliant on India's manufacturing base) would need to grow significantly to realize the overall growth targets, and these sectors should be prioritized accordingly. Some of the promising product areas for exports are discussed below.

7.1 Project Exports

Project exports are broadly defined as exports of such goods and services where the export receipts are allowed to be staggered (in conformity with RBI guidelines) over a period of more than 12 months. This is largely to reflect that the export transaction is not a one-off single transaction but represents certain goods, construction and service activities, where the payment receipts are staggered in line with the project components/execution.

Many Indian companies in both the private and public sectors have, over the years, developed considerable expertise in executing project export contracts in diverse areas such as railway sector, power sector, roads and bridges, drinking water supply schemes, irrigation projects, construction of oil and gas pipelines, construction of electricity grids, hydro power projects, airport construction etc.

Project exports have evolved over recent years to: (a) reflect India's technological maturity and industrial capabilities, (b) give visibility to Indian technical expertise and project execution capability and (c) create entry points for other Indian firms for supplies, consultancy and manpower exports. There is a growing realisation across Asia and Africa that the experience of Indian companies is more appropriate to their project needs, especially in hydro-power, irrigation, transportation and water supply systems. Indian exporters need to make inroads into the lucrative markets in West Asia, including Iraq and Libya. There is also the need to secure sub-contracts from major European, American and Japanese companies.

The challenges for Indian project exports can be listed as follows:

1. Relatively lower ability to compete with many other countries, including developed ones and China, in the absence of competitive credit.
2. Lack of experience in handling barter deals and counter-trade practices.
3. Low levels of effective and strategic tie-ups with reputed international consultancy firms and quality accreditation.

Some important initiatives have been taken to promote project exports. Guarantee by Government of India for repayment of principal and payment of interest has facilitated offer of competitive credit. Bid Intervention Service by Exim Bank [2], on behalf of Indian companies, seeks redressal in case of discrimination against Indian companies in multilateral tenders. EXIM Bank has so far intervened in 32 bid intervention cases, of which 19 were successful with contracts ultimately going in favour of Indian companies.

7.2 Information Technology (IT) Sector

The adoption of one of the most liberal trade and investment regimes in the IT sector has given the country a highly efficient system in basic telecommunications. Liberalisation of trade in high technology goods and the development of efficient basic telecommunication through opening up of the sector have brought India to the forefront of developing nations supplying IT-enabled and knowledge-related services. If India can continue to produce engineers and highly skilled categories of professionals, it can hope not only to maintain its position but also increase its standing in the world knowledge economy.

Studies suggest that growth will be driven by more traditional outsourcing service lines—such as hardware and software maintenance, network administration and help desk services—and not lines such as application development and management (ADM) and R&D services.

Achieving high growth in software exports will require deep and enduring innovation across multiple dimensions like: (a) business model innovation, (b) focus on new service lines (like infrastructure off-shoring and knowledge innovation), (c) developing Internet Protocol based solutions, (d) systematic talent enhancement, (e) better technology and (f) research capabilities.

Some of the key challenges which need to be overcome include: (a) documenting procedures and establishing performance benchmarks, (b) addressing concerns around data security, (c) improving the workforce quality and skills and (d) continuously innovating and developing new service lines along with improved operational excellence.

Within IT, relative to software and services sector, IT hardware has lagged far behind. One of the reasons for the under-investment in IT sector is the slow development of the hardware sector. With the implementation of Information Technology Agreement in April 2005, there are zero duties for the ITA 1 items and greater international competition for the hardware sector. IT production development has to focus on the combined hardware-software sector and production for domestic sector along with exports.

Trade in services is uncharted territory with plenty of opportunities and challenges. A more conducive environment for trade in services can be created by liberalizing FDI in services as FDI inflows and trade in services have a close relationship given the nature of intra-firm trade of multinational parent firms with affiliates. Rationalizing taxation of services, streamlining domestic regulations like licensing requirements and procedures, and regulatory transparency can help in the growth and export of services.

7.3 Services Sector

Exports of services resulting in a surplus in services trade have contributed significantly to partially bridging the merchandise trade deficit. In particular, net software exports have grown significantly. However, the external environment suggests that despite efforts to boost exports, there is likely to be a challenging environment for growth of services. In such a scenario, it is absolutely essential to address some of the critical supply side bottlenecks which have been impeding India's export performance in services.

Foremost would be the need to improve regulations and legal framework governing some of key service sectors, such as engineering, architecture, accountancy, legal, health-related services, software, construction, audio-visual, wholesale and retail trade, education, environment and financial services.

The services sector has emerged as a prominent sector in India in terms of its contribution to national and State incomes, trade flows and FDI inflows. The sector contributes around 58 percent to the GDP of the country and 28 percent to employment. Its contribution to total trade is 25 percent, around 35 percent to exports and 20 percent to imports. The sector accounts for more than 50 percent of FDI into the country. The services sector in India has in general grown at a rate higher than the overall GDP growth rate.

7.4 Gems and Jewellery

Another important labour intensive export sector that must continue to be encouraged is that of gems and jewellery. This sector has relatively low value addition, but contributes a high volume of exports and employment and is, therefore, important. The gems and jewellery manufacturing sector largely consists of small and medium enterprises (SMEs), employing skilled and semi-skilled labour, almost entirely in the unorganized sector. This sector is not only a major source of revenue generation but also a source of employment, employing a skilled workforce of 35 lakh. The gems and jewellery sector is an import-intensive sector with export orientation. It also requires high working capital.

The top five export destinations for Indian gem and jewellery products are UAE, Hong Kong, US, Belgium and Israel. The sector has been included under the Make in India initiative.

7.5 Pharmaceutical Industry

Pharmaceutical industry (including biotech) has done really well in establishing a global reputation for quality products. There is an opportunity for India to become *pharmacy of the world.* So far, pharma exports have been dominated by generics and prospects for expansion in this segment are good. Developed economies are facing fiscal problems and wherever public health is a major charge on the national exchequer, governments will have to rely upon high quality generics instead of patented or brand-named drugs. This is an opportunity India cannot miss.

The pharmaceutical sector is beset with several challenges. Most of these challenges arise out of the enviable reputation of India as a reliable supplier of generic medicines. These challenges include the following:

1. Campaigns to malign generic products as being in violation of India's intellectual property rights (IPRs)

commitments.

2. Alleged lack of compliance of generic medicines coming out of India, with quality standards.
3. India's over dependence on some sources for its active pharmaceutical ingredients (APIs).
4. India not being party to the Pharmaceutical Inspection Convention and Pharmaceutical Inspection Co-operation Scheme and therefore Indian Pharmacopeia not being recognized yet in major markets.
5. India's pricing policies forcing Indian exporters to price their products with extremely low margins.

7.6 Engineering Goods

In spite of huge growth of Indian engineering sector in recent years, the industry is suffering from severe technological obsolescence and lack of economies of scale. This is because 40 percent of India's engineering exports are in the micro, small and medium enterprises (MSMEs) sector which is exporting low value added products due to constraints on financial capacities to invest in technology and research and development. There is need to concentrate on exports of high value added items. For this purpose it is important for the MSME sector to upgrade its technology to enable it to move up the value chain.

Technology upgradation would involve use of state-of-the-art technology by the MSMEs which would improve productivity, and/or quality of products. It would also bring about use of environment-friendly or green technology that would substantially improve the working environment.

7.7 Chemicals

Although India is supplier of quality chemicals at most competitive price in the world, it does not have its own Chemical Inventory and Chemical Management Programme. Chemical Inventory is a listing of industrial chemicals in commerce manufactured or imported by a country. It is primarily used to distinguish between new and existing chemicals. It is a data base created from information submitted to government authorities by manufacturers, processors, users, and importers. If put in place, it will help India's chemical management programme. It will also help in implementing other regulatory compliances.

7.8 Electronics Goods

Electronics goods sector is characterized by a large variety of products which are imported and exported as well. There is a huge domestic demand for electronics products which is met largely by imports and some local manufacture. Large and rising domestic demand fuelled by the growing middle class has resulted in companies not actively looking for export opportunities.

The Indian electronic hardware manufacturers also experience a higher level of taxation, cost of power, finance and freight and poorer infrastructure compared to their competitors from China, Taiwan, Korea and Japan. Consequently the cost of production of most electronic goods in India is at least 8 to 10 percent higher than in other countries of Southeast Asia.

China, India's main competitor in this sector, with its state-of-the-art infrastructure and manufacturing competitiveness has an even bigger advantage. It is, therefore, not surprising that China has been able to attract large market leaders in the electronics sector with established international brands by offering land at low cost, high quality infrastructure that reduces transaction costs, low wages, subsidized credit and extremely liberal capital structure.

This has led to economies of scale which, in turn, have made the Chinese electronic goods industry competitive. A strategy to enhance exports of electronic goods from India will have to address the disabilities vis-à-vis China and leverage competitive advantage.

Indian exports of electronics hardware can increase faster

if exports of high value added items increase and export basket is diversified. The strength of Indian electronics industry in design, system integration and diagnostic skills needs to be leveraged for catering to niche markets. While some interventions will have major impacts in the long-term, if implemented effectively, they will make a difference sooner.

7.9 Leather Products

The leather sector is amongst the top 10 foreign exchange earners for the country. Extensive capacity expansion will be critical to realize the full potential for future growth of the leather industry.

Even though the impressive growth witnessed by the leather sector is encouraging, there are several factors which pose a great challenge to the sector in the future. These include competition not only from China and other Southeast Asian Countries but also from countries like Pakistan and Bangladesh, and the rising prices of chemicals/inputs required by the leather/tanning industry.

Leather sector is a major employment creating sector. India already has a significant name in the footwear sector. Additional focus is required for composite leather footwear exports as well as leather garment manufacturing and exports and non-leather product exports. The sector also needs financial resources to augment its environmental compliance.

Therefore, attention should be paid to the following:

1. Greater focus on finished and composite products.
2. Additional attention to garments, non-leather products.
3. Improving competitiveness through supporting environmental compliance expenses and other capital expenses.
4. Supporting skill development and marketing efforts.

7.10 Textiles

In textiles, India needs to realize more effectively the scope for growth made possible since the dismantling of the quota regime. The labour intensity of the apparel industry is one of the highest. With over 45 million people employed directly, the apparel industry is one of the largest sources of employment in India. As a net exporter of cotton yarn, India has an advantage over competitors such as China and Bangladesh and can benefit from moving up the value chain. Product diversification in garments is essential; into women's garments, value added cotton products, and synthetic textiles. In these sectors, the aim should be to scale up operations and increase export growth rates.

The textiles and garments sector has traditionally been a leader of India's exports in global markets particularly to the traditional markets of the US and EU. While it continues to be an important sector, it has come up against several challenges. The textiles policy should address most of the concerns of this sector. As far as the foreign trade policy is concerned, it recognizes the employment creation potential of this sector. It also recognises the importance of the apparel sector particularly as a value creator and as an employment generator. India is positioned along the entire value chain of cotton and synthetic textiles and garments.

It needs to reorient itself in view of increasing global challenges and emerging opportunities. Several developing countries are becoming major competitors of India in the garments sector. India must, therefore, leverage its capacity in the pre-garment stages of the value chain while it should add unique value to the garment stage of the value chain. Further, it must regionalise its value chain in a manner that a continuum is established within the region.

7.11 Carpets

India ranks number one in terms of value as well as in volume of exports of handmade carpets. The major competition to the export of Indian handmade carpets comes from China, Iran, Nepal and Pakistan.

The industry has a huge potential for growth. India has around 29 percent share of the world market for handmade carpets and floor coverings. US is the largest importer accounting for about 50 percent of the total exports.

It is a well-known fact that the cycle of carpet production from the date of receipt of order till the date of shipment is very long (6 to 12 months). Also carpet production is done over a huge geographical area. Therefore, it is important that methods be devised to compensate the industry from the high transaction costs to make it competitive against its foreign counterparts.

Infrastructure needs to be improved in the major carpet clusters particularly Bhadohi/Mirzapur belt. This may include improvement of roads, power supply and provision of better medical facilities to the weavers.

Carpet export sector is heavily dependent on US and European Markets. Effort should be made to explore new markets, e.g. Turkey, and Middle East.

7.12 Iron Ore

A few years ago, iron ore exports used to comprise a large part of India's exports to China and several other markets. Today, for several reasons, iron ore exports have dwindled to a trickle. The recent lifting of the ban on iron ore mining in some States will unshackle iron ore mining activity. At the same time India is embarking upon a programme of manufacturing for which iron ore would be required at home. In the last few years, pelletisation facilities have also come up in a major way in the country. All this will mean that iron ore exports may not reach the same levels as was the case a couple of years ago. This is particularly true in the context of exports to China where growth rates have declined reducing the demand for iron ore. Nevertheless, as global markets pick up, it is expected that iron ore exports, particularly as pellets, will increase.

Efforts at increasing value-addition within the country would be required, so that, unlike as at present, more finished products based on iron ore rather than raw material are exported, e.g. pelletization of iron ore fines.

7.13 Agriculture Exports

In a country like India, with a population of 121 crore (Census 2011) and agriculture largely depending on the vagaries of monsoon, any strategy to promote agricultural exports will necessarily have demand and supply factors at its core, with instruments of procurement, storage and distribution to service the same. The periodic and recurrent spurts in the prices of essential commodities do not augur well for exports. It is, therefore, essential to have a clear policy about foodgrains based on the buffer norms and strict implementation of the same. As for the perishable products like fruits and vegetables, the country should have a system whereby critical reserves could be procured and stored at strategic locations by a centralized agency to ensure that any unusual rise in the price of a perishable essential commodity can be offset by prompt delivery of sufficient quantities to control the prices.

Such centrally procured stocks of perishable commodities if unutilised for price stabilization, can then be offloaded in the retail market or exported where possible with or without processing before the new harvest of that product comes into the market. This system will need to be fine-tuned to ensure availability of essential commodities at reasonable prices in the domestic market and at the same time continue with sustainable exports to remain a credible supplier in the international market.

To sum up, it is expected that the future export drivers for India will be textiles, engineering goods, including automobiles and capital goods and processed food items. Textiles have long been a traditional export item for India accounting for nearly one-fifth of the total exports during the 1990s. With the phasing out of the Multi-Fibre Arrangement (MFA) and dismantling of quotas from January 1, 2005, the potential for India's textile exports is likely to increase significantly. India's advantage in textile production, which is labour intensive, lies in its competitive advantage in labour, raw materials including cotton and low import intensity.

However, the textile industry has, to a large extent, been reserved for the small scale industry, with the entry of the organised sector not permitted until recently. This has led to fragmentation of the sector leading to lack of economies of scale, low productivity, weak quality control and technological obsolescence. To tap the potential, the textile industry requires significant technological upgradation, scale building and a shift in focus from low value fabric exports to high value apparels and garments.

Endnotes

1. Department of Commerce, Ministry of Commerce and Industry, Government of India (2010), *Strategy for Doubling Exports in Next Three Years (2011-12 to 2013-14).*
2. Established in 1982, Export-Import Bank (EXIM Bank) operates as a co-ordinating agency in the field of international finance and for the development of merchant banking activities in export-oriented industries.

8

Region-wise and Country-wise Export Strategy

8.1 Region-wise Export Strategy

8.1.1 European Union (EU): EU, as a regional bloc, is India's largest trading partner. EU is a highly discerning market. It presents several challenges in the area of sanitary and phytosanitary standards and technical standards, complex systems of quotas and tariffs and trade remedial actions against Indian products. The EU's practice of constantly evolving its sanitary and phytosanitary standards and procedures is a major challenge and raises the bar for exports from developing countries.

While India's merchandise exports in some sectors are very well integrated with the EU market, there is significant potential for growth in many of the employment creating sectors. There is also high potential for growth of exports in technology areas such as automobiles, auto components, engineering products and pharmaceuticals. Therefore, EU continues to be an important market. India has been the beneficiary of the GSP in some sectors. [1] However, some of these sectors have now been excluded from the EU GSP list adversely impacting India's market access for these products.

EU is also a significant market for India's information technology services but India has not been able to adequately harness the potential because of the data security related constraints thrown up by EU regulations. While large Indian companies can respond to EU's data security framework, smaller companies find it impossible to access the EU market. India's skilled professionals find the EU regime for movement of natural persons for services delivery highly discomforting, and expensive. India's services particularly in the IT and ITES sector have contributed to the competitiveness of several US businesses. A similar approach is available to the EU companies if these challenges are appropriately addressed.

8.1.2 Southeast Asia: In pursuance of the 'Look East Policy', which has been a major pillar of the country's foreign policy since the early 1990s, India has developed multi-faceted relationship with ASEAN countries both bilaterally and multilaterally. Taking this to the logical next phase, the 'Act East Policy' of the Government of India endeavours to cultivate wide-ranging economic and strategic relations in South-East Asia.

The ASEAN-India Trade in Goods Agreement, which was signed in Bangkok on August 13, 2009, entered into force on January 1, 2010. The ASEAN-India Agreement on Trade in Services and Investment was concluded in 2014 and will become operational from July 1, 2015.

It provides business certainty to service providers from both India and ASEAN countries and is expected to strengthen business and commercial relations between ASEAN and India. It will also open up opportunities of movement of both manpower and investments between India and ASEAN.

The India-Singapore Comprehensive Economic Cooperation Agreement became operational from August 1, 2005. A Comprehensive Economic Cooperation Agreement was signed with Malaysia on February 18, 2011. A Comprehensive Free Trade Agreement is being negotiated with Thailand.

8.1.3 Africa: There is enormous untapped potential for enhancing India's economic relations with the African continent, encompassing not just trade and investment but also capacity development, technical assistance and provision of services such as healthcare and education. India shares several commonalities with the countries in this region in terms of high economic growth rates, large domestic markets, a young demographic profile and abundant natural resources.

Agro-processing, manufacturing, mining, textiles, fast moving consumer goods (FMCG), infrastructure development and construction can offer huge potential to Indian companies.

India has already stepped up its assistance in Africa and intends to further increase aid-for-trade assistance in the coming years. The private sector both in Africa and in India see India's development assistance as having a comparative advantage in many services sectors, including information technology, education, vocational skills development, health and financial services.

Facilitating investment by private Indian entrepreneurs, especially in agriculture, in Africa is another means to build productive capacity and generate employment there while bringing about greater integration between the major African economies and India. Greater cooperation in agriculture and agro-processing would also contribute to food security in both Africa and India.

A small but significant step taken by India is a 3-year technical assistance programme for the cotton sector which is underway for 6 African countries and is in the final year of implementation. The response to this programme has been extremely positive and the Government is looking to expand this programme both in terms of its scope and coverage. Further, there is tremendous scope for India to help African countries, especially less developed countries, to augment their capacity in international trade policy and law as well as to provide sector-specific training for expanding trade.

There is enormous untapped potential for enhancing India's economic relations with the African continent, encompassing not just trade and investment but also capacity development, technical assistance and provision of services such as healthcare and education. Agro-processing, manufacturing, mining, textiles, infrastructure development and construction are highly promising areas for Indian companies. India is engaging actively with countries and regional groupings in Africa for trade agreements, project exports and capacity building initiatives.

8.1.4 Commonwealth of Independent States (CIS): Trade between India and the CIS region—which includes 12 countries, namely Kazakhstan, Turkmenistan, Uzbekistan,

Kyrgyzstan, Tajikistan, Russia, Georgia, Azerbaijan, Armenia, Ukraine, Belarus and Moldova—has increased in recent years. Russia and Ukraine are India's major trading partners in this region.

CIS region offers enormous market potential given its strong GDP, high per capita incomes and the abundance of natural resources such as petroleum, coal, natural gas, potash, fertilizers, metals and minerals. The CIS region has a strong complementarity with India's manufacturing sector.

8.1.5 Latin America: Brazil is India's major trade partner in the region. Brazil and India are both members of BRICS, IBSA and the G20. India's other important trading partners in the region are Venezuela, Argentina, Chile, Columbia and Peru. India's export basket, except in respect of Brazil, is largely dominated by commodities such as crude oil, iron ore, copper, sugar, soya, cereals etc.

8.2 Country-wise Export Strategy

8.2.1 US: US is one of India's top trading partners and now that the US is back on a growth path, future bilateral trade prospects are bright. Employment-generating sectors such as textiles, agriculture, leather and gems and jewellery should continue to receive major attention for promoting exports to the US market. Important aspects of the India-US economic relationship for India include access for India's high-skilled professionals in US markets, and increased investment. Regular dialogue with the US to make India's perspective clear on issues such as intellectual property rights, immigration policies of the US Government, labour and skill related policies of the US Government, should also be a key part of the India-US economic relationship.

8.2.2 Japan: Japanese market has not seen growth in the product areas of India's interest. Moreover, Indian business entities are facing problems in market access. These problems can be briefly said to be arising out of language constraints faced by Indian companies in Japan. Highly demanding product and service standards make market access a costly venture. India's trade and investment relationship with Japan is unique in nature. Japan is India's largest investment partner. Several ongoing initiatives in this direction are likely to increase Japanese investment in India. Indian business would, therefore, have the option of taking part in this process of investment generated trade.

The other route of access of India's export sectors into Japan will require language proficiency, negotiating a simplified framework for market access and continuous trade promotion efforts on the part of businesses and the Government. The Government should, therefore, run special programmes for trade promotion in Japan in identified sectors such as textiles, garments, information technology services, pharmaceuticals, leather products and agro processed products.

8.2.3 Russia: Invigorating trade and investment ties with Russia is a focus area of the Government. India's trade with Russia, a member of the WTO since 2012 and a BRICS partner, remains surprisingly small.

There are several complementarities between the two sides and scope to increase cooperation in areas such as hydrocarbons, nuclear energy, pharmaceuticals, fertilizers, diamonds, coking coal, agro products, textiles and leather, engineering, information technology services and infrastructure development.

Some of the impediments faced by exporters in trading with Russia include the following:

1. Underdeveloped trade infrastructure.
2. Onerous regulatory requirements.
3. Complex and time-consuming customs procedures.
4. Requirement for the exporter to bear the cost of obtaining import licences.
5. Product-specific approvals.
6. Pre-shipment inspection.
7. Frequent changes in laws, decrees and regulations.
8. Complicated rules for certification of products.
9. Banking and finance issues.

In addition, Indian exporters face various non-tariff barriers in their trade with Russia such as stringent sanitary and phytosanitary standards on bovine meat, egg products, oilseeds and non-basmati rice. The Indian pharmaceutical industry also faces similar barriers in exporting to Russia.

8.2.4 China: India's most important trading partner amongst the countries of North East Asia is China. Engagement with China requires a comprehensive approach on trade, investment and economic cooperation issues. India should continue to pursue market access issues and removal of non-tariff barriers on India's exports of pharmaceuticals and agro commodities. It should seek to obtain market access for Indian IT services and encourage other service sectors such as tourism, film and entertainment. Furthermore, India should look for Chinese investment in boosting domestic manufacturing capacities, while remaining vigilant against any unfair trade practices.

Commenting on the diversification of India's foreign trade, *Economic Survey,* 2011-12 observed, "India has made progress in diversifying its export and import markets. The share of Asia and the Association of South East Asian Nations (ASEAN) in total trade increased from 33.3 percent in 2000-1 to 57.3 percent in the first half of 2011-12, while that of Europe and America fell from 26.8 percent to 19 percent. This has helped India weather the global crisis emanating from Europe and America. The USA has been displaced by the UAE as India's largest trading partner, followed by China, since 2008-9". [2]

In order to put exports on a high growth trajectory, India needs a market diversification strategy based on the changing dynamics of growth in the world economy. So far India's bilateral trade engagement has been mainly with the industrial powers or driven by multiple considerations. In future engagements, India will engage with regions and countries that are not only promising markets but are also major suppliers of critical inputs and have complementarities with the Indian economy.

While there has been a gradual shift in India's exports away from the advanced economies of the European Union and North America, the United States of America continues to be the topmost destination for India's exports.

Diversification of exports and the development of new export markets should be viewed as part of a wider effort to enlarge the country's foreign trade and expand commercial and economic relations with other countries. In the coming years special attention should be given to the development of close economic relations with other developing regions, notably South and South East Asia.

Endnotes

1. EU's Generalised Scheme of Preferences (GSP) allows developing country exporters to pay less or no duties on their exports to the EU. This gives them vital access to EU markets and contributes to their economic growth. On January 1, 2014, the new GSP preferences started to apply. This reformed GSP focuses support on developing countries most in need.
   There are three main variants (arrangements) of the scheme:

- The standard/general GSP arrangement, which offers generous tariff reductions to developing countries. Practically, this means partial or entire removal of tariffs on two thirds of all product categories.
- GSP+enhanced preferences means full removal of tariffs on essentially the same product categories as those covered by the general arrangement. These are granted to countries which ratify and implement international conventions relating to human and labour rights, environment and good governance.
- Everything but Arms (EBA) arrangement for least developed countries (LDCs), which grants duty-free quota-free access to all products, except for arms and ammunitions.

2. Government of India, *Economic Survey,* 2011-12, p. 14.

9

Export Promotion Councils (EPCs)

Export Promotion Councils (EPCs) are an important instrumentality for the promotion and development of the India's exports. Each Council is responsible for the promotion of a particular group of products, projects and services. The main role of the EPCs is to project India's image abroad as a reliable supplier of high quality goods and services. In particular, the EPCs are tasked with encouraging and monitoring the observance of international standards and specifications by exporters. They are also required to keep abreast of the trends and opportunities in international markets for goods and services and assist their members in taking advantage of such opportunities in order to expand and diversify exports.

EPCs have, over time, acquired a central position in India's trade promotion efforts. They are under the administrative control of the Department of Commerce, Ministry of Commerce and Industry, Government of India. EPCs are registered as non-profit organizations under Societies Registration Act or the Companies Act. They perform both advisory and executive functions. Almost all of them receive trade promotion grants from the Department of Commerce.

9.1 Engineering Export Promotion Council (EEPC)

Way back in 1955-56, the nascent Indian engineering sector was in the process of diversifying and restructuring the narrow export base of the industry and it needed a strong push. EEPC was set up in 1955 under the sponsorship of Ministry of Commerce, Government of India, for export promotion of engineering goods, projects and services from India. Initially started with a few hundred engineering units as a small outfit, it has grown to be the largest Export Promotion Council having membership of nearly 12,000 from amongst large corporate houses, Star Trading Houses, small and medium scale units, trading houses etc.

Engineering exports from India have been steadily growing and the performance has probably exceeded all expectations ever since the birth of EEPC. Apart from being one of the largest stakeholders in the total exports of India, the engineering exporters are the foremost net foreign exchange earner for the country. As the engineering sector is extremely diversified, EEPC has set up different product panels with a view to ensure that all possible and potential Indian products reach out to the global markets.

EEPC aggressively peruses a number of activities and services for its exporting community, its members and the potential overseas buyers with a two-point objective of facilitating exports of Indian engineering products and services to the global market and to provide the overseas buyers true value.

9.2 Project Exports Promotion Council of India (PEPC)

PEPC is an export promotion council which was set up in 1984 (as Overseas Construction Council of India). PEPC in line with the Foreign Trade Policy of the Government of India not only undertakes the necessary export promotion initiatives but also provides necessary technical information to set up overseas projects in any of the following modules of engineering service:

1. Civil construction (structures/infrastructure).
2. Turnkey.
3. Process and engineering consultancy services.
4. Project construction items (excluding steel and cement)/project goods.

9.3 Chemicals and Allied Products Export Promotion Council (CAPEXIL)

CAPEXIL, a non-profit making organization, was set up in

March 1958 by the Ministry of Commerce, Government of India to promote exports of chemical and allied products from India. With headquarters in Kolkata, and regional offices in New Delhi, Mumbai, Kolkata and Chennai, CAPEXIL has more than 4,500 members across the country. One of the fascinating aspects of CAPEXIL is the overwhelming variety of products it deals with.

CAPEXIL sends trade delegations to all major and developing markets around the world, showcasing Indian exports all over the world through exhibitions and fairs. It can help the sourcing needs of an importer anywhere in the world, and also the selling needs of Indian exporters.

CAPEXIL is an ISO 9001: 2000 certified organization.

9.4 Council for Leather Exports (CLE)

CLE is the single largest and apex trade promotion organisation of the strong and rapidly growing Indian leather and leather products industry. CLE is committed towards the overall development of Indian leather sector and achieve higher export growth to enhance India's share in global leather trade. It is the notified export promotion organization for the entire leather and leather products industry.

9.4.1 Core Objectives of CLE: These are as under:

1. Develop and strengthen the leather industry, both industrial development as well as export growth.
2. Undertake concerted and aggressive export promotion and market development activities to extend global reach of Indian leather and leather products.
3. Assist importers anywhere in the world towards their sourcing needs of Indian leather and leather products.
4. Provide necessary assistance/guidance to overseas entrepreneurs in establishing business collaborations and strategic alliances with Indian companies.
5. Serve as a vital link between the Government and the leather industry, representing important policy measures, focusing on overall health and growth of the entire sector.

9.4.2 Activities and Services of CLE:

1. Disseminating market information, trends, policy matters and publishing information on commercial, technical and technological developments in the Indian leather industry.
2. Facilitating export-import trade through redressal of various procedural hurdles by representing to authorities concerned.
3. Participating in major international leather trade fairs and specialized trade shows across the globe.
4. Organizing buyer-seller meets and mega leather shows.
5. Promoting, facilitating and attracting joint ventures, technical collaborations and strategic alliances.
6. Inviting resource persons/experts to the trade fairs, seminars and workshops held in India, for exchange of information, knowledge, ideas and strategies.
7. Mooting delegations to overseas countries with a view to identify the sources for raw materials for augmenting availability of leather for production in India.
8. Performing facilitation and coordination activities towards implementation of various leather sector infrastructure strengthening, human resource development programmes of Government of India.

9.5 Sports Goods Export Promotion Council (SGEPC)

SGEPC, a Government of India sponsored organization, is working for the promotion of India's exports of sports goods and toys. Founded in 1958, SGEPC represents all the leading manufacturers and exporters of sports goods and toys in India.

SGEPC is managed by a Committee of Administration (COA), which consists of elected representatives from the Indian industry and includes two Government representatives. The one point objective of SGEPC is to promote exports of sports goods and toys from India. SGEPC's range of activities include: (a) spurring the industry's performance and (b) promoting its presence internationally.

SGEPC is a common platform for companies from all over

the country, with common interests, where they can meet to exchange views, decide on common strategies for promotion and also wherefrom they can voice their concerns at both national and international levels.

SGEPC organizes trade promotion activities like Indian participation in international trade fairs, visits of business delegations, promotional campaigns in international markets etc.

SGEPC provides important information to the members on market intelligence, standards and specifications, quality and design, and on any other issue which may directly or indirectly affect the industry.

SGEPC is the direct link between the industry and the Government whereby it provides feedback on industry's requirements to the Indian Government and also informs Government directives to the industry.

SGEPC collects export data from its members, maintains a statistical record of exports of sports goods and toys and evaluates its performance on an annual basis. SGEPC recognizes the achievements of exporters and awards the top performers annually.

9.6 Gem and Jewellery Export Promotion Council (GJEPC)

GJEPC was set up by the Ministry of Commerce, Government of India in 1966. It was one of several Export Promotion Councils (EPCs) launched by the Indian Government to boost the country's export thrust, when India's post-Independence economy began making forays in the international markets. Since 1998, the GJEPC has been granted autonomous status.

GJEPC is the apex body of the gems and jewellery industry and presently it represents almost 6,000 exporters in the sector. With headquarters in Mumbai, GJEPC has regional offices in New Delhi, Kolkata, Chennai, Surat and Jaipur, all of which are major centres for the industry. It thus has a wide reach and is able to have a closer interaction with members to serve them in a direct and more meaningful manner.

Over the years, GJEPC has emerged as one of the most active export promotion councils and has continuously strived to expand its reach and depth in its promotional activities.

Various promotional activities undertaken by the GJEPC, over the years, have significantly and positively impacted the increase of exports of gems and jewellery from India.

GJEPC's promotional activities include organising a number of important trade shows held in the country like the India International Jewellery Show (IIJS), Signature IIJS, India Gem and Jewellery Machinery Expo (IGJME). The IIJS is the largest gems and jewellery fair in the country and amongst the foremost internationally. It attracts visitors and buyers from all across the country and from several countries in the world. Signature IIJS was set up as a boutique show and has gone on to develop its own niche. IGJME, a more recent addition to the bouquet of shows, filled in an important gap—a trade fair totally devoted to technology—thereby enabling companies in the field to access the cutting edge developments in the field in a convenient manner.

GJEPC, on occasions, ties up with other government bodies for special initiatives. The India Gems and Jewellery Fair, for example, was organised in New Delhi in 2013 as a joint venture with the India Trade Promotion Organisation (ITPO). GJEPC has also tied up in the past with the Ministry of Tourism for jewellery promotions on international platforms.

The India International Jewellery Week is a jewellery fashion extravaganza highlighting the design capabilities of the jewellery industry, attracting both fashion enthusiasts and buyers from India and abroad. Various region-specific buyer-seller meets, and delegations to important gems and jewellery centres in other parts of the world, are some of the other trade promotion activities undertaken by GJEPC.

GJEPC produces a spectrum of published and digital material both as part of its various activities as well as standalone publications. These include Solitaire magazine and various brochures and event-specific publications and websites for all its main activities, events and projects. It also advertises its activities and highlights the industry in international media throughout the year.

As the singular apex body of the gems and jewellery export industry in India, GJEPC is the voice of the industry, taking its issues to the government and seeking appropriate measures for resolving them. It has been mandated by the Government of India as the nodal agency for the Kimberley Process Certification Scheme (KPCS), and plays a key role in maintaining the data and paperwork of the flow of all diamonds certified as “conflict-free” going in and out of the country.

A crucial aspect of the GJEPC’s functioning relates to various measures undertaken to upgrade, upskill and generally improve the industry’s standards and products. It has set up various institutes across the country, foremost among them being the Indian Institute of Gems and Jewellery (IIGJ) imparting international quality courses for training artisans and designers for this industry. Various gemmological institutes under its umbrella—like the Gemmological Institute of India (GII), Gem Testing Laboratory, Jaipur, Indian Gemmological Institute, New Delhi and Indian Diamond Institute (IDI) in Surat—undertake research, training and certification activities. IDI was established as a Society in the year 1978 with the objective of enhancing the quality, design and global competitiveness of the Indian jewellery.

GJEPC interacts closely with the National Skill Development Council (NSDC), an initiative of the Government of India, to take the latter’s programme to the gems and jewellery industry. It has played an important role in setting up the Gem and Jewellery Skill Council of India (GJSCI) recently.

Regular seminars and conferences organised by GJEPC impart knowledge about latest developments or issues in related fields. From time to time, it has also undertaken campaigns and held seminars to encourage companies to follow the highest standards in business practices and ethics, thereby maintaining the best standards in the industry.

Taken together, through its various functions and activities, GJEPC has helped to forge a fitting atmosphere to provide a boost for gems and jewellery exports.

9.7 Shellac and Forest Products Export Promotion Council (SHEFEXIL)

Shellac Export Promotion Council (SEPC) was formed in 1957 under the sponsorship of Ministry of Commerce and Industry, Government of India, to facilitate India's exports of shellac and lac-based products.

In 2005, SEPC's role was enhanced as the nodal export promotion council for India's non-timber forest produce, to facilitate exports of veg saps and extracts, guar gum, sesame seeds, herbs, niger seeds, other vegetable materials, fixed vegetable oil, cakes and more. Subsequently, SEPC was renamed as SHEFEXIL (Shellac and Forest Products Export Promotion Council) and it now supports 860 individual products.

In 2007, SHEFEXIL was declared as the nodal export promotion council for the North-Eastern Region of India, to facilitate all exports from the states of Assam, Arunachal Pradesh, Manipur, Nagaland, Meghalaya, Tripura, Mizoram, and Sikkim.

Mission: SHEFEXIL is run by a tri-directional mission to:

1. Strengthen plans and initiatives for exports of non-timber forest produce.
2. Maximize India's export potential through collective action.
3. Assist the members of the Council to boost exports and discharge their responsibilities and obligations under Foreign Trade Policy.

Vision:

4. To realize the full potential of India's non-timber forest produce exports through collective action.
5. To create a global brand for Indian non-timber forest produce.

6. To conceptualize plans and initiatives for exports of non-timber forest produce.
7. To turn exports of non-timber forest produce as a tool for improving the lives of the poorer section of the population and develop the economically weaker sections of the society.
8. To boost employment-oriented non-timber forest produce exports and ensuring infrastructure development in rural/ tribal areas.

9.7.1 SHEFEXIL's North-East Mandate:

SHEFEXIL is a direct contributor to economically challenged sections of society—tribal women and marginal cultivators of North-East areas. It is active with a multi-faceted role to

1. Grant RCMC to multi-product exporters having head office or registered office in the North-East Region.
2. Oversee exports from the North-East Region.
3. Organize export promotion activities to boost exports from the North-East Region.
4. Undertake developmental activities to enhance exports from the North-East Region.
5. Highlight all constraints and barriers to enhance exports from North-East Region to all policy making bodies.
6. Contribute towards policy making at the national level on all matters relating to unlocking the potential of the North-East Region.

North-East Region is a paradise waiting to be touched by prosperity. It is richly endowed with forest products, and SHEFEXIL and North-East have a symbiotic relationship to offer excellent potential for exports of minor forest produce. With 98 percent of its borders forming India's international boundaries with China, Bangladesh, Myanmar and Bhutan, it has strong potential to become an international market base. North-East India is also poised to convert into a strategic base for foreign and domestic investors to tap the vast contiguous markets of Southeast Asia and East Asia—China, Malaysia, Thailand, Singapore, Philippines, Indonesia and other Far East Asian countries.

9.8 Cashew Export Promotion Council (CEPC)

Four centuries ago, the adventurous Portuguese came sailing down the Indian coasts and brought with them the priceless tree nut *cashew*, the wonder nut of the world. It took deep roots in the entire coastal region of India. Cashew found the Indian soil more homely than its homeland. Later it spread as a popular crop to other parts of India. Cashew cultivation now covers a total area of 0.70 million hectares of land, producing over 0.40 million metric tonne of raw cashewnuts annually. Cashew tree is a short, stocky, low-spreading, evergreen tropical tree. It flowers once a year, between the months of November and January. The fruit ripens fully within 2 months.

The nuttiest feature of cashewnut is that it is attached to the lower portion of the cashew apple which looks like a fruit, but in reality it is the enlarged stem of the cashew tree. Cashewnut can be seen sitting smugly under the soft belly of the cashew' apple. Together, it is one of the fascinating sights of nature.

Cashewnut seed has within itself a whole kernel and this delicate kernel is covered by a testa membrane and a thick outer shell which effectively protects the tasty kernel from the ravages of nature from the time of harvesting to processing.

In its raw form, cashew kernel is soft, white and meaty. When roasted it changes colour and taste. Cashew kernel turns from a creamy white into a golden hue and the mellow pulp becomes crisp. Salted, it appeals to the palate as the most delicious nut.

India was the first country to hit the world market with cashew kernels and it was she who pioneered cashew processing as an industry. India is the largest producer, processor and exporter of cashews in the world.

The raw cashew nuts collected from the growing areas are moved to the factories for processing. It is ensured that the raw nuts are thoroughly cleaned and are free from all foreign matter before they are taken for processing.

Cashew Export Promotion Council of India (CEPC) was established by the Government of India in 1955, with the active cooperation of the cashew industry with the object of promoting exports of cashew kernels and cashewnut shell liquid from India. By its very set up, ECPC provides the necessary institutional framework for performing different functions that serve to intensify and promote exports of cashew kernels and cashewnut shell liquid. It provides the necessary liaison for bringing together foreign importers with member exporters of cashew kernels. The enquiries received from the foreign importers are circulated amongst its members.

CEPC also extends its good offices in settling complaints amicably in matters of exports/imports either on account of quality and/or variation in fulfilment of contractual obligations. It undertakes publicity abroad with a view to projecting the *product image* which serves to highlight and focus attention on the high quality and superiority of Indian cashews. It participates in specialised international food fairs/exhibitions and general fairs abroad. As it represents the whole industry, it arranges display of products received from members free of cost. The enquiries received are circulated amongst the members for them to contact the parties abroad for business negotiations.

9.9 Plastics Export Promotion Council (PLEXCONCIL)

PLEXCONCIL represents the exporting community in the Indian plastics industry. The export promotion strategies evolved since 1955, the year when PLEXCONCIL was born, have fetched rich dividends, which is exhibited in the form of high export growth rates. These achievements represent the dedicated efforts of the about 2,200-strong PLEXCONCIL members who are always in the process of creating a niche for themselves in the world markets by virtue of their determination to achieve technological excellence, and a sense of commitment to satisfy their customers' requirements. PLEXCONCIL supports the efforts of its members to achieve export excellence and service the overseas buyers to find appropriate trade partners in the Indian plastic industry.

In its pursuit to achieve export excellence, various export promotional activities are undertaken by PLEXCONCIL. These include participation in international trade fairs, sponsoring delegations to target markets, inviting business delegations from overseas to India, organising buyer-seller meets and servicing the needs of its members.

9.10 Pharmaceuticals Export Promotion Council (Pharmexcil)

The main objectives of Pharmexcil are as follows:

1. To support, protect, maintain, increase and promote the export of drugs and pharmaceuticals including, inter alia, intermediates, herbal, ayurvedic, unani and homeopathic medicines, biotech and biological products, diagnostics, surgicals, nutraceuticals, pharma industry related services. It also promotes collaborative research, contract manufacturing, providing base for clinical trials and consultancy.
2. To keep communication with chambers of commerce and other mercantile and public bodies through out the world with a view to taking appropriate and necessary measures for maintaining or increasing the exports of drugs and pharmaceuticals.
3. To enunciate just and equitable principles to govern the trade in drugs and pharmaceuticals and to set up codes of practices for the general guidance of manufacturers, traders and exporters of these products and further to simplify transactions relating to their exports.
4. To advise or represent to governments, local authorities and public bodies concerning: (a) policies and other measures, including direct and indirect taxation, adopted

by them in relation to their effect on industry and (b) steps to be taken by them to prevent any contravention of the codes of practices laid down by Pharmexcil.

9.10.1 Services Rendered by Pharmexcil:

1. Organizing trade delegations/buyer-seller meetings.
2. Assisting members to get their MDA/MAI claims refunded from Government of India.
3. Dissemination of trade enquiries received from abroad.
4. Issue of certificate of origin.
5. Organizing periodical seminars/interactive meetings on exports-related issues.
6. Make suggestions to Government of India on policy issues relating to pharma exports
7. Make representations to Government of India and other agencies in India and abroad to get amicable solutions for the common problems of the industry.

Products and services falling under purview of Pharmexcil include bulk drugs and its intermediates, formulations, herbal, ayurvedic, unani, siddha and homeopathic medicines, biotech and biological products, diagnostics, surgicals, neutraceuticals, and pharma industry related services like collaborative research, contract manufacturing, clinical trials and consultancy.

9.11 Services Export Promotion Council (SEPC)

Services sector is playing a pivotal role in the growth of Indian economy and employment generation, and has become oiling wheel of the growth and prosperity of Indian masses. Over the years, services exports have constantly been giving trade surplus for India. Service sector has shown higher growth rate as compared to agriculture and manufacturing sectors. Service sector is the largest and fastest growing sector in the Indian economy making as high as 59 percent contribution in total GDP of India.

SEPC, an export promotion council set by Ministry of Commerce and Industry, Government of India, is an apex trade body to facilitate service exporters of India and serving as a platform of interaction between service exporters and policy makers. SEPC has been instrumental in promoting the efforts of Indian service exporting community.

SEPC has been mandated to promote export of services in the following sectors:

1. Healthcare services.
2. Legal services.
3. Accounting and auditing services.
4. Hotel and tourism-related services.
5. Environmental services.
6. Entertainment services.
7. Maritime transport-related services.
8. Distribution services.
9. Architectural services.
10. Educational services.
11. Advertising services.
12. Consultancy services.
13. Marketing services.
14. Printing and publishing services.

To sum up, Export Promotion Councils should play a leading role in studying overseas markets and maintaining up to date intelligence. It is also necessary to strengthen the existing arrangements for enabling India's commercial representatives in foreign countries to provide adequate intelligence regarding overseas markets and to make these available to Indian industry and trade and, generally, to promote the country's foreign trade as intensively as possible.

10

Special Economic Zones (SEZs)

SEZs are intended as engine for economic growth supported by quality infrastructure, with minimum possible regulations, and an attractive fiscal package, both at the level of Central and State Governments.

Various incentives and facilities are offered to both SEZ developers and units in SEZs for attracting investments, including foreign investment, into SEZs. These incentives and facilities are expected to trigger a large flow of foreign and domestic investment in SEZs, in infrastructure and productive capacity, leading to generation of additional economic activity and creation of employment opportunities.

10.1 Special Economic Zones Act, 2005

India was one of the first in Asia to recognize the effectiveness of the export processing zone (EPZ) model in promoting exports, with Asia's first EPZ set up in Kandla (Gujarat) in 1965. However, the EPZs were not able to emerge as effective instruments for export promotion on account of multiplicity of controls and clearances, absence of world-class infrastructure and an unstable fiscal regime.

Considering the need to enhance foreign investment and promote exports from the country and realising the need that level playing field must be made available to the domestic enterprises and manufacturers to be competitive globally, the special economic zones (SEZs) Policy was announced in April 2000. This policy intended to make SEZs an engine for economic growth supported by quality infrastructure complemented by an attractive fiscal package, both at the Centre and the State level, with the minimum possible regulations. SEZs in India functioned from November 1, 2000 to February 9, 2006 under the provisions of the Foreign Trade Policy and fiscal incentives were made effective through the provisions of relevant statutes.

To instil confidence in investors and signal the Government's commitment to a stable SEZ policy regime and with a view to impart stability to the SEZ regime thereby generating greater economic activity and employment through the establishment of SEZs, a comprehensive draft SEZ Bill was prepared after extensive discussions with the stakeholders. The Special Economic Zones Act, 2005, was passed by Parliament in May 2005 which received Presidential assent on June 23, 2005. After extensive consultations, the SEZ Act, 2005, supported by SEZ Rules, came into effect on February 10, 2006, providing for drastic simplification of procedures and for single window clearance on matters relating to Central as well as State Governments. The main objectives of the SEZ Act are the following:

1. Generation of additional economic activity.
2. Promotion of exports of goods and services.
3. Promotion of investment from domestic and foreign sources.
4. Creation of employment opportunities.
5. Development of infrastructure facilities.

The SEZ Act, 2005 envisages key role for the State Governments in export promotion and creation of related infrastructure. A single window SEZ approval mechanism has been provided through a 19 member inter-ministerial SEZ Board of Approval (BoA). The applications duly recommended by the respective State Governments/UT Administrations are considered by BoA periodically. All decisions of the BoA are with consensus.

The SEZ Rules provide for differentiated minimum land requirement for different classes of SEZs. Every SEZ is divided into a processing area where alone the SEZ units would come up and the non-processing area where supporting infrastructure is to be created. The SEZ Rules also provide for simplified procedures for development, operation and maintenance of the SEZ, setting up units in SEZs, single window clearance both relating to Central as well as State Governments for setting up of an SEZ and units in a SEZ, and simplified compliance procedures/documentation with emphasis on self-certification. A Board of Approval has been constituted by Government in exercise of the powers conferred under the SEZ Act.

SEZs in India seek to promote value addition component in exports, generate employment and mobilize foreign exchange. SEZs when operational are expected to offer high quality infrastructure facilities and support services, besides allowing for the duty free import of capital goods and raw materials. Additionally, attractive fiscal incentives and simpler customs, banking and other procedures are offered in such zones. Setting up of SEZs is also treated as an infrastructure development activity and offered same incentives. SEZs in India closely follow the Chinese model.

SEZs are intended as engine for economic growth supported by quality infrastructure, with minimum possible regulations, and an attractive fiscal package, both at the level of Central and State Governments.

Various incentives and facilities are offered to both SEZ developers and units in SEZs for attracting investments, including foreign investment, into SEZs. These incentives and facilities are expected to trigger a large flow of foreign and domestic investment in SEZs, in infrastructure and productive capacity, leading to generation of additional economic activity and creation of employment opportunities.

10.2 Approval Mechanism and Administrative Set up of SEZs

10.2.1 Approval Mechanism: The developer submits the proposal for establishment of SEZ to the concerned State Government. The State Government has to forward the proposal with its recommendation within 45 days from the date of receipt of such proposal to the BoA. The applicant also has the option to submit the proposal directly to the BoA.

BoA has been constituted by the Central Government in exercise of the powers conferred under the SEZ Act. All the decisions are taken in the BoA by consensus. BoA has 19 Members. It is headed by the Secretary, Department of Commerce in the Ministry of Commerce and Industry, Government of India.

10.2.2 Administrative Set Up: The functioning of the SEZs is governed by a three- tier administrative set up. BoA is the apex body and is headed by the Secretary, Department of Commerce. The Approval Committee at the Zone level deals with approval of units in the SEZs and other related issues. Each Zone is headed by a Development Commissioner, who is ex-officio chairperson of the Approval Committee.

Once an SEZ has been approved by the BoA and Central Government has notified the area of the SEZ, units are allowed to be set up in the SEZ. All the proposals for setting up of units in the SEZ are approved at the Zone level by the Approval Committee consisting of Development Commissioner, Customs Authorities and representatives of State Government. All post-approval clearances including grant of importer-exporter code number, change in the name of the company or implementing agency, broad banding diversification etc. are given at the Zone level by the Development Commissioner. The performance of SEZ units is periodically monitored by the Approval Committee and units are liable for penal action under the provision of Foreign Trade (Development and Regulation) Act, 1992 in case of violation of the conditions of the approval.

10.3 Criteria for Approval

Proposals for setting up SEZ in the public/private/joint/State sector are required to meet the following conditions.

1. Minimum size of the SEZ shall not be less than 1,000 hectares. This would however, not apply to existing EPZs

converting into SEZs as such or for notifying additional area as a part of such SEZ or to product-specific port/airport based SEZs.

2. SEZ and units therein shall abide by local laws, rules, regulations or bye-laws in regard to area planning, sewerage disposal, pollution control and the like. They shall also comply with industrial and labour laws and such other laws/rules and regulations as may be locally applicable.
3. SEZs shall make adequate arrangements to fulfil all the requirements of the laws, rules and procedures applicable to such SEZs.
4. Only units approved under the SEZ scheme would be permitted to be located in SEZ.

Proposals received for setting up of SEZs are considered by an Inter-Ministerial Committee known as the Board of Approval (BoA), in its meeting held every month. The promoters of the SEZs are also invited to such meetings to explain the salient features of their proposals and to furnish clarifications, wherever required.

Proposals that are received up to 15 days prior to the scheduled meeting of the Board of Approval are placed for its consideration and any proposals received thereafter are considered in the next meeting.

10.4 Conversion of EPZs into SEZs

10.4.1 How are SEZs Different from EPZs? In one sense, SEZs are only a variant of EPZs. Both have delineated area and enjoy duty free import of capital goods and raw materials. Both aim to attract foreign investment for setting up export-oriented units by providing developed infrastructure, conducive operating environment and a package of fiscal incentives.

However, the objectives of SEZs are much larger than mere promotion of export processing activities. While EPZs are industrial estates, SEZs are virtually industrial townships that provide supportive infrastructure such as housing, roads, ports and telecommunications. The scope of activities that can be undertaken in the SEZs is much wider and their linkages with the domestic economy are stronger. Consequently, they have a diversified industrial base. Their role is not transient like that of EPZs, as they are intended to be instruments of regional development as well as export promotion. As such, SEZs can have tremendous impact on exports, inflow of foreign investment and employment generation.

Indian EPZs have not fared well as these are so few and their areas are small. For some, the location is inappropriate and they are subject to cumbersome procedures for long. However, in many East Asian economies, EPZs have been highly successful in their initial phase of opening up. Therefore, the mere fact that India is switching over to the SEZ model may not per se guarantee success as demonstrated by China unless policy parameters and implementation strategy are planned carefully.

Some of the existing EPZs have been converted into SEZs. For example, the Government has converted EPZs located at Kandla and Surat (Gujarat), Cochin (Kerala), Santa Cruz (Mumbai-Maharashtra), Falta (West Bengal), Chennai (Tamil Nadu), Visakhapatnam (Andhra Pradesh) and NOIDA (Uttar Pradesh) into SEZs.

10.4.2 Will EPZ Conversion Help? The proposal to convert existing EPZs into SEZs does not make much sense, because their size and infrastructure will remain the same. It is only the customs regime envisaged for SEZs which is sought to be superimposed on them, though not favoured by the entrepreneurs in some of the EPZs. Unless there is a demand from entrepreneurs for switch over to the SEZ regime, it should not be forced upon them. China has only five SEZs but a variety of other EPZ type zones which have a slightly different policy framework. In the hinterland and in backward areas, India may have to rely on smaller EPZ type zones, as it is not possible to set up SEZs everywhere, having regard to the availability of skills and social and economic infrastructure.

10.5 Incentives and Facilities Offered to Units in SEZs

The incentives and facilities offered to the units in SEZs for attracting investments into the SEZs, including foreign investment, include the following:

1. Duty free import/domestic procurement of goods for development, operation and maintenance of SEZ units.
2. 100 percent income tax exemption on export income for SEZ units under Section 10AA of the Income Tax Act for first 5 years, 50 percent for next 5 years thereafter and 50 percent of the ploughed back export profit for next 5 years.
3. Exemption from minimum alternate tax under Section 115JB of the Income Tax Act.
4. External commercial borrowing by SEZ units up to US$ 500 million in a year without any maturity restriction through recognized banking channels.
5. Exemption from Central Sales Tax.
6. Exemption from service tax.
7. Single window clearance for Central and State level approvals.
8. Exemption from State sales tax and other levies as extended by the respective State Governments.

10.6 Incentives and Facilities Available to SEZ Developers

These include the following:

1. Exemption from customs/excise duties for development of SEZs for authorized operations approved by the BoA.
2. Income tax exemption on income derived from the business of development of the SEZ in a block of 10 years in 15 years under Section 80-IAB of the Income Tax Act.
3. Exemption from minimum alternate tax under Section 115 JB of the Income Tax Act.
4. Exemption from dividend distribution tax under Section 115O of the Income Tax Act.
5. Exemption from Central Sales Tax (CST).

6. Exemption from Service Tax.

10.7 Apprehensions and Concerns

Concerns have been expressed regarding acquisition of agricultural land for setting up SEZs. The State Governments have been advised that in land acquisition for SEZs, first priority should be for acquisition of waste and barren land and if necessary single crop agricultural land could be acquired for the SEZs. If perforce a portion of double cropped agricultural land has to be acquired to meet the minimum area requirements, especially for multi-product SEZ, the same should not exceed 10 percent of the total land required for the SEZ. Various issues relating to setting up of SEZs in the country including issues raised by various political parties are being addressed by the Empowered Group of Ministers.

Some of the apprehensions against the SEZs are the following:

1. Generation of little new activity as there may be relocation of industries to take advantage of tax concessions.
2. Revenue loss.
3. Large-scale land acquisition by the developers which may lead to displacement of farmers with meagre compensation.
4. Acquisition of prime agricultural land having serious implications for food security.
5. Misuse of land by the developers for real estate.
6. Uneven growth aggravating regional inequalities.

Many of these apprehensions, however, can be addressed through appropriate policies and safeguards.

10.8 SEZs and National Security

SEZs coming up in different parts of India have raised security concerns in government circles, particularly the Home Ministry. Government is reluctant to allow any SEZ near the border, fearing threat to national security. All zones with a port or near an existing dock are being closely watched. However, the government-owned Kandla Port Trust, which is setting up a ₹ 7,300 crore port-based zone, has been allowed to proceed further with the project. Similarly, doubts are being raised about gems and jewellery SEZs on the ground that operating units could smuggle precious metals and stones in and out of the country. Furthermore, pharmaceutical industry is also on the watch list. The Home Ministry wants a stricter dispensation for companies undertaking DNA-related work in the SEZs.

In short, Government's thinking in clear on the subject, i.e. country's security is paramount and any unit in a SEZ could be shut down the moment it is found to be indulging in anything that is detrimental to national interest.

10.9 Lessons from China

10.9.1 Size of SEZ: Chinese SEZs are like townships. India has not gone that far, but it is heartening that realising that size does matter, the government has decided to have large-sized SEZs. According to the guidelines, the area of an SEZ should be 1,000 hectares. This reflects a sea change in the Government's perception. The best performing EPZ in Mumbai has an area of 93 acres only. It hardly needs reiteration that only a large-sized zone can generate economic activity on some reasonable scale. In a small zone, the requisite infrastructure and services cannot be provided nor can multiple economic activities be promoted.

The SEZs proposed to be set up at Positra in Gujarat, Navi Mumbai in Maharashtra, Nanguneri in Tamil Nadu, Kakinada in Andhra Pradesh, Paradeep in Odisha, Kapri in West Bengal, Bhadoi in Uttar Pradesh and Indore in Madhya Pradesh are much bigger than the existing EPZs, though compared to the Chinese SEZs, their size is small.

10.9.2 Customs Regulations: The customs regime in Chinese SEZs provides tremendous operational ease. The customs regulations designed for Indian SEZs also seem to be far less cumbersome than those for EPZs. The entrepreneurs will be free from routine inspections of import-export cargo. Procedures for operations such as record keeping, inter-unit transfer, sub-contracting and disposal of obsolete material and waste and scrap will be simpler. Enterprises will be allowed to utilise duty free raw materials over five years. These changes will definitely make the customs regime investor friendly.

10.9.3 Incentives Package: The incentive package in India is quite liberal and may even be a shade better than that for Chinese SEZs. In fact, it is more or less on par with the package for the existing EPZs. Duty free import of capital goods and raw materials, reimbursement of Central sales tax, tax holiday for specified period, 100 percent repatriation of profits for subcontracting facilities are allowed. The Government has done well by extending incentives for the infrastructure sector to zone developers and the units as well. This can attract foreign direct investment for providing internationally competitive infrastructure.

Thus, so far as the size of SEZs, their customs regime and incentive package are concerned, the Indian policy compares quite favourably with the Chinese policy framework. However, in relation to the regime of labour laws, decentralisation of powers in favour of State Governments and the duty structure for DTA access, it falls short of expectations.

10.9.4 Labour Laws: As regards labour laws, it is difficult to imagine that a communist country like China has relaxed these laws by allowing a hire and fire policy for the SEZs. This single measure went a long way in attracting foreign investment to these zones. After investors gained confidence in the productivity of Chinese workforce, the hire and fire policy was substituted by the contract system. There is ample justification for adopting in India a flexible labour policy, at least for these exporting enclaves, on the ground that they are exposed to uncertain international market conditions, recession or rejection of consignments. On the positive side, they create gainful additional employment and facilitate inflow of foreign investment. The policy in India on this critical issue is lukewarm in as much as it states that the laws of the land will apply and that the zones can be declared as public utilities under the Industrial Disputes Act. Merely declaring SEZs as public utilities will, however, not serve much purpose as is borne out by the EPZ experience.

10.9.5 Involvement of State and Local Authorities: China made the provincial and local authorities partners and stakeholders by delegating them powers for approving foreign investment. The SEZ authorities in China can approve investment proposals up to US$ 30 million. This has been a significant feature of the Chinese policy and a key contributor to the success of SEZs. The Indian policy only enables the State Governments to set up SEZs, but does not empower them to approve investment proposals. These powers have been vested with the development commissioners concerned who represent the Central Government. This will result in centralisation of work in their offices.

Unless the State Governments are directly made responsible for the management of SEZs and approving investment proposals, their political leadership and bureaucratic set up may not have any incentive to push the initiative forward. Their cooperation and active participation in the drive for setting up SEZs is essential. China has gone a step further by delegating powers to the local authorities. The local authority manages Shenzhen SEZ, which has the highest export turnover. India needs to do likewise.

Some additional measures will be necessary to deepen and widen the interface with the State Governments and attract foreign investment. As States were not associated in the past with export promotion activities, they have little idea of what is required to be done. For their meaningful participation, they need to have role clarity and a sense of identification with the scheme. They should fully comprehend the details of the SEZ model for proper micro planning at their end.

10.9.6 DTA Sales: Another ticklish issue relates to domestic market access for units in the SEZs. The proposed policy of levying full import duty on DTA sales does not seem to be right in view of the current differentials in the effective rates of import and excise duties. This will bar the entry of units based on indigenous inputs into SEZs since such sales will not be viable for them. The SEZs will only attract import intensive investment with low net foreign exchange earnings. Though China has set up a variety of zones, the infrastructure and incentive package for SEZs were the most attractive. For Indian SEZs, this may not be the case in so far as domestic market access is concerned. For a country of India's size, domestic market access is an important issue for investors in SEZs. In the Chinese SEZs, about 50 percent production is sold in the DTA.

10.9.7 Foreign Investment and Technology: The thrust of SEZs in China was on attracting foreign investment and technology and that should also be the prime concern in India. This is not possible without aggressive marketing and promotion. Zone managements in China wooed investors aggressively and provincial and local authorities competed with each other to attract investors.

10.10 Issues Relating to SEZs

10.10.1 Goods and Services Tax (GST): As per the GST model being considered, GST will be levied on imports with necessary constitutional amendments. Though full and complete set off would be available on the GST paid on import of goods and services, after the introduction of the GST, tax exemptions, remissions, etc. related to industrial incentives should be converted, if at all needed, into cash refund schemes after collection of tax, so that the GST scheme on the basis of a continuous chain of set-offs is not disturbed. Regarding special Industrial Area Schemes, such exemptions, remissions would continue up to legitimate expiry time both for the Centre and the States. However, any new exemption, remission, or continuation of an earlier one would not be allowed. In such cases, the Central and State Government could provide reimbursement after collecting the GST.

10.10.2 Power Generation and Distribution: Another

area of concerns is the generation and distribution of power by the SEZ developers/units. While one opinion is that it should be left to the entrepreneur to decide whether he would like to provide power as an infrastructure, as defined in the SEZ Act, or set up a unit to sell power as a good, another view is that power cannot be an infrastructure and can be only a good to be generated and distributed by the unit. It may be worth considering appropriate policy to encourage power generation and distribution.

10.10.3 Dual Control and Co-ordination: The Directors, STPI, have been declared development commissioners (DCs) for the IT SEZs under their respective jurisdiction. An STPI is under administrative control of the Department of Information Technology. Other multi-product and sector-specific SEZs are under the charge of DCs appointed by the Department of Commerce. However a number of issues, for example processing of notification of IT SEZs, coordination with state governments etc, relating to IT SEZs are also looked after by the DCs appointed by the Department of Commerce. This leads to a situation of dual control adversely impacting effective coordination and needs to be resolved.

10.10.4 Disinvestment: The new SEZs have come up mainly in the private sector with no funding from the Government. Now the time has possibly come to see whether some of the established SEZs which are state owned could also be privatized. Disinvestment in these SEZs could not only add to the kitty of the Government and release more money for social-sector development but could also make these SEZs more efficient.

To sum up, the recent initiative of the Government of India to set up SEZs on the pattern of China is a welcome change in the strategy for economic development and export promotion. The move is a bold departure and a paradigm shift in the basic approach to development efforts. It is an acknowledgement of the potential of export-led development strategy.

SEZs have been set up in various parts of the country in

the private sector, as joint ventures and also by the State Governments. However, this new approach to development is facing resistance in some of the States, particularly from the farming community which is accusing the government of forcibly taking over fertile land from them at heavily discounted prices as against the prevailing market prices.

As the things stand, SEZs are coming up in a select few States which are offering various concessions and facilities to private entities. The already lagging-behind States are not receiving much attention from private developers. This might sharpen regional inequalities as was experienced after the green revolution of late 1960s and early 1970s.

The challenge ahead lies in appropriately sequencing to sustain the popular support for reforms and reconciling the conflicting interests of the various reforms constituencies. The recent debate about SEZ indicates the kind of considerations that have to be taken into account in the formulation of policies. While the initiative on SEZs is laudable, its success will depend on how well the model is evolved and the implementation strategy worked out.

The task ahead is to examine how far the key policy parameters that contributed to the success of SEZs in China have been incorporated in the Indian policy framework. The distinguishing features of Chinese SEZs are their large size, investment friendly customs regime, flexible labour laws, liberal policy for DTA access, attractive package of incentives and delegation of powers in favour of provinces and local authorities for managing the zones.

The process of decentralisation needs to be taken to its logical conclusion by empowering local authorities and State Governments to approve investment proposals. The Central and State Governments should market SEZs aggressively to attract foreign investment. Relaxation of labour laws and rationalisation of duty on DTA access can give a big boost to the scheme.

To sum up, India's Export Processing Zone Scheme,

launched in 1965, was the precursor to the present day SEZ (Special Economic Zones) Scheme. The SEZ Act was enacted in 2005 and made operational through SEZ Rules in February 2006. The objectives of the SEZ Scheme, as laid out in Section 5 of the SEZ Act, are as follows: (a) promotion of exports of goods and services, (b) promotion of investment from domestic and foreign sources, (c) creation of employment opportunities and (d) development of infrastructure facilities.

Underlying the enactment of the SEZ Act was the need to provide long-term stability and continuity to the scheme. In order to achieve this objective, income-tax provisions were incorporated in the Act. However, in 2011, minimum Alternate tax (MAT) and dividend distribution tax (DDT) were imposed on the SEZs, which has severely hampered the progress of the SEZ scheme.

The SEZ scheme, in terms of export promotion through tax incentives, is not unique to India. Such schemes continue to be in operation in some form or other in several countries.

11

Exports and Goods and Services Tax (GST)

11.1 Goods and Services Tax (GST): Brief Introduction

India introduced a comprehensive Goods and Services Tax (GST) on July 1, 2017. Prior to the introduction of GST, the indirect tax system of India suffered from various disabilities. There was a burden of *tax-on-tax* in the pre-GST system of Central excise duty and the sales tax (later VAT) system of the States.

GST is a tax on goods and services with comprehensive and continuous chain of set-off benefits up to the retailer level. It is essentially a tax only on value addition at each stage, and a supplier at each stage is permitted to set-off, through a tax credit mechanism, the GST paid on the purchase of goods and services. Ultimately, the burden of GST is borne by the end-user (i.e. final consumer) of the commodity/service.

GST is a comprehensive indirect tax levy on manufacture, sale and consumption of goods as well as services at the national level. GST is an indirect tax for the whole of India to make it one unified common market. GST is designed to give India a world class tax system and improve tax collections. It has ended the long-standing distortions of differential treatment of manufacturing sector and services sector. GST has facilitated seamless credit across the entire supply chain and across all States under a common tax base.

Since major Central and State indirect taxes have got subsumed under GST, the multiplicity of taxes has been substantially reduced which, in turn, would decrease the operating costs of the country's tax system. With GST in place, the burden of Central sales tax (CST) has also been removed. The uniformity in tax rates and procedures across the country will go a long way in reducing compliance costs.

There are three components of GST so far as intra-state trade is concerned.

1. Central Goods and Services Tax (CGST).
2. State Goods and Services Tax (SGST).
3. Union Territory Goods and Services Tax (UT-GST).

Another important component of GST is Integrated Goods and Service Tax (IGST) which is levied by the Centre on inter-state supply of goods or services or both. IGST rate is broadly equal to CGST rate plus SGST rate. SGST component of IGST accrues to the consumer state.

Similarly, a compensation cess on certain specified goods is imposed to compensate States for any revenue loss on account of implementation of GST.

11.2 Meaning of Export of Goods and Services

According to Section 2(5) of the IGST Act, 2017, "export of goods means taking goods out of India to a place outside India". [1]

As per Section 2(6) of the same Act, "export of services means the supply of any service when:

1. the supplier of service is located in India;
2. the recipient of service is located outside India;
3. the place of supply of service is outside India;
4. the payment for such service has been received by the supplier of service in convertible foreign exchange; and
5. the supplier of service and the recipient of service are not merely establishments of a distinct person in accordance with Explanation 1 in Section 8.

11.3 Exports are Inter-state Supplies

Section 7 of the IGST Act, 2017, comprehensively defines the term *inter-State supply.* As part of the comprehensive definition of inter-state supply, Section 7(5) of the Act treats the supply of goods/services as inter-state supply: (a) when the supplier is located in India and the place of supply is outside India and (b) when supply is made to or by a special economic zone (SEZ) developer or a SEZ unit.

11.4 Exports are Zero-rated Supplies

What is zero-rated Supply? Zero rated supply is a supply of goods/services on which no tax is payable but input tax credit pertaining to that supply is admissible.

All exports (whether of goods or services) as well as supplies to SEZs have been categorized as zero-rated supplies in the IGST Act. [2]

Zero-rated supply under Section 16(1) of the IGST Act, 2017 means any of the following supplies of goods/services namely:

1. Export of goods or services or both; or
2. Supply of goods or services or both to a SEZ developer or a SEZ unit.

The concept of zero rating of supplies requires the supplies as well as the inputs used in supplying the supplies to be GST-free. This is ensured by employing the following means:

1. Taxes paid on the supplies which are zero-rated are refunded.
2. Credit of input taxes is allowed.
3. Wherever the supplies are exempted, or the supplies are made without payment of tax, the tax paid on inputs (i.e. unutilized input tax credit) is refunded.

As per Section 16(2) of the IGST Act, 2017 credit of input tax may be availed for making zero-rated supplies, notwithstanding that such supply may be an exempt supply.

Thus, even if a supply is exempted (e.g. sanitary napkins), the credit of input tax may be availed for making zero-rated supplies.

Explanation to Section 54 of the CGST Act, 2017 defines refund as under:

"*refund* includes refund of tax paid on zero-rated supplies of goods or services or both or on inputs or input services used in making such zero-rated supplies, or refund of tax on the supply of goods regarded as deemed exports [3], or refund of unutilised input tax credit as provided under sub-section (3)". [4]

11.4.1 Compensation Cess: It is a cess levied under Section 8 of the Goods and Services Tax (Compensation to States) Act, 2017. It is applicable—in addition to the regular GST taxes (CGST + SGST/UT-GST on intra-state supplies and IGST on inter-state supplies—on the supply of certain notified goods/services. The following goods—which mostly belong to the luxury and demerit categories—have been notified for the purpose so far.

1. *Pan masala.*
2. Tobacco and tobacco products.
3. Coal.
4. Aerated waters.
5. Motor vehicles.

The rate of compensation cess varies for different notified goods. It is imposed to compensate states for any revenue loss on account of implementation of GST.

Compensation cess is not charged on goods exported by an exporter under bond and the exporter is eligible for refund of input tax credit of cess relating to goods exported. In case goods are exported on the payment of cess, the exporter is eligible for refund of cess paid on goods exported by him, along with refund of input tax credit of cess relating to goods exported.

11.5 Options for the Exporters

According to Section 16(3) of the IGST Act, 2017, "A registered person making zero rated supply shall be eligible to claim refund under either of the following options, namely: (a) he may supply goods or services or both under bond or Letter of Undertaking…without payment of integrated tax and claim refund of unutilised input tax credit; or (b) he may supply goods or services or both…on payment of integrated tax and claim refund of such tax paid on goods or services or both supplied, in accordance with the provisions of section 54 of the Central Goods and Services Tax Act or the rules made thereunder".

A registered person making zero-rated supply can claim refund under either of the following options.

1. Export under bond [5] or letter of undertaking (LUT) [6] without payment of tax.
2. Export along with tax payment and claim refund later.

Any registered taxpayer exporting goods can make use of LUT. However, any person who has been prosecuted for tax evasion for an amount of ₹ 2.5 crore or more under the GST laws is not eligible to furnish LUT. The validity of such LUT is for a period of 1 year (till the end of financial year). An exporter furnishing LUT is required to furnish fresh LUT for each financial year. If the conditions mentioned in LUT are not satisfied within the time-limit, the privileges are revoked and the exporter will have to furnish bond.

For all the other assesses (including the ones who have been prosecuted for tax evasion of ₹ 2.5 crore or more under the GST laws), bond is to be furnished if the export is being made without payment of IGST.

11.6 Grant of Provisional Refund in Case of Zero-rated Supplies

Section 54(6) of the CGST Act, 2017 provides for grant of provisional refund of 90 percent of the total amount of refund claimed, on account of zero-rated supply of goods/services by a registered person. The remaining 10 percent can be refunded later after due verification of documents furnished by the applicant.

Provisional refund would be paid within 7 days after giving the acknowledgement. The acknowledgement of refund application is normally issued within a period of 14 days but in case of refund of integrated tax paid on zero-rated supplies, the acknowledgement would be issued within a period of 3 days.

The amount of provisional refund is credited directly to the claimant's bank account.

There is a condition attached to provisional refunds. The provisional refund is not granted if the applicant has been prosecuted for any offence under the GST law or earlier law within past 5 years. The amount of tax evaded in such prosecution shall be more than ₹ 2.5 crore.

11.7 Refund Problems

Refund is the main problem of exporters. Twenty-second meeting of the GST Council held on October 6, 2017, provided a comprehensive relief package for exporters.

Government has organized special refund drives for exporters from time-to-time. Dedicated refund cells and help desks have been established in each commissionerate to help exporters to get their refund claims processed.

However, there are procedural problems and delays in getting refunds because export documents are to be verified and refund claims passed. Because of this delay, the working capital of the exporters gets blocked which adversely affects their capacity to export.

11.8 Failure to Export Goods and Services

What happens if goods and services are not exported? The provisions laid in Rule 96A of the CGST Rules, 2017 in this regard are as under:

(1) Any registered person availing the option to supply goods or services for export without payment of IGST shall furnish, prior to export, a bond or a letter of undertaking binding himself to pay the tax due along with interest:

(a) if goods are not exported outside India within 3 months of issuing the export invoice. The tax shall be paid within 15 days from the end of such three months period, or

(b) if the payment for goods is not received in convertible foreign exchange within one year. The tax shall be paid within 15 days from the expiry of such one year.

(2) The details of the export invoices furnished on the common portal shall be electronically transmitted to the system designated by Customs and a confirmation that the goods covered by the said invoices have been exported out of

India shall be electronically transmitted to the common portal from the said system.

(3) Where the goods are not exported within the time specified in sub-rule (1) and the registered person fails to pay the amount mentioned in the said sub-rule, the export as allowed under bond or letter of undertaking shall be withdrawn forthwith and the said amount shall be recovered from the registered person in accordance with the provisions of Section 79 of the CGST Act, 2017.

(4) The export as allowed under bond or letter of undertaking withdrawn in terms of sub-rule (3) shall be restored immediately when the registered person pays the amount due.

(5) Authorities, by way of notification, may specify the conditions and safeguards under which a letter of undertaking may be furnished in place of a bond.

(6) The provisions of sub-rule (1) shall apply, mutatis mutandis, in respect of zero-rated supply of goods or services or both to a SEZ developer or a SEZ unit without payment of integrated tax.

11.9 Export of Goods and Services to Nepal and Bhutan

In GST law, export of goods and export of services are treated differently. As already noted, definition of *export of goods* under Section 2(5) of the IGST Act, 2017 attaches no condition other than 'taking goods out of India to a place outside India'. However in case of export of services, Section 2(6) of the same Act mandates, *inter alia*, the receipt of payment in *convertible foreign exchange*.

In case export proceeds from Nepal and Bhutan are received in Indian rupees, they will qualify as export in terms of goods but not in terms of services. If the payment is not received in freely convertible currency, then such services will not be treated as exports and in such situations the service provider has to discharge the tax liability.

Consequent upon the recommendations made by the GST Council in its Twenty-third meeting held in Guwahati on

November 10, 2017, services to Nepal and Bhutan are treated as export of services irrespective of realization of payment in Indian Rupee. Such services are exempt from payment GST and allowed ITC.

In short, goods and services exported to Nepal and Bhutan are exports, irrespective of realization of payment in India rupee.

11.10 Refund of IGST Paid on Supply of Goods to Tourist Leaving India

According to Section 15, "The integrated tax paid by tourist leaving India on any supply of goods taken out of India by him shall be refunded in such manner and subject to such conditions and safeguards as may be prescribed.

Explanation—For the purposes of this section, the term "tourist" means a person not normally resident in India, who enters India for a stay of not more than six months for legitimate non-immigrant purposes".

Endnotes

1. Section 2(56) of the CGST Act, 2017 defines *India* to means the territory of India as referred to in Article 1 of the Constitution, its territorial waters, seabed and sub-soil underlying such waters, continental shelf, exclusive economic zone or any other maritime zone as referred to in the Territorial Waters, Continental Shelf, Exclusive Economic Zone and other Maritime Zones Act, 1976, and the air space above its territory and territorial waters.
   While territorial waters extends to a distance of 12 nautical miles into sea from the nearest point of the appropriate baseline, the Continental Shelf extends beyond the limit of the territorial waters to the outer edge of the continental margin or to a distance of 200 nautical miles from the baseline. Similarly, Exclusive Economic Zone is an area beyond and adjacent to the territorial waters, and the limit of such zone is 200 nautical miles from the baseline. Accordingly, it may be inferred that the jurisdiction of GST law would extend to 200 nautical miles into sea.
2. In its Twelfth Meeting held on March 16, 2017, the GST Council cleared a proposal for the zero rate to be applied for

goods and services going to special economic zones (SEZs). In other words, supplies made to SEZs are zero-rated and considered as physical exports. In the earlier decision—in case of procurement of supplies by SEZs—tax was to be paid and then refund claimed of such tax paid but as per the discussion in the said meeting the same supplies were accepted as zero-rated.

3. As per Section 2(39) of the CGST Act, 2017, "*deemed exports* means such supplies of goods as may be notified under Section 147". According to section 147 of the same Act, "The Government may, on the recommendations of the Council, notify certain supplies of goods as deemed exports, where goods supplied do not leave India, and payment for such supplies is received either in Indian rupees or in convertible foreign exchange, if such goods are manufactured in India".
4. Sub-section (3) of Section 54 of the CGST Act, 2017 states, "...a registered person may claim refund of any unutilised input tax credit at the end of any tax period: Provided that no refund of unutilised input tax credit shall be allowed in cases other than: (i) zero-rated supplies made without payment of tax; (ii) where the credit has accumulated on account of rate of tax on inputs being higher than the rate of tax on output supplies (other than nil rated or fully exempt supplies), except supplies of goods or services or both as may be notified by the Government on the recommendations of the Council: Provided further that no refund of unutilised input tax credit shall be allowed in cases where the goods exported out of India are subjected to export duty: Provided also that no refund of input tax credit shall be allowed, if the supplier of goods or services or both avails of drawback in respect of central tax or claims refund of the integrated tax paid on such supplies".
5. **Bond:** It has a surety (another person) who guarantees the performance on the part of the obligor (person furnishing the bond).
6. **Letter of Undertaking (LUT):** It is a type of bank guarantee, under which a bank allows its customer to raise money from another Indian bank's foreign branch as a short-term credit.

12

Export Promotion Strategy, Issues and Concerns

India's exports have recorded considerable improvement since the initiation of the reform process in early 1990s. At the same time, it is also clear that export performance of the country has not been able to fully utilise the potentials. High transaction costs and low levels of factor productivity are some of the factors, which are often cited as reasons for less than satisfactory export performance by the country.

In this context, NITI Aayog had observed, "Why do exports matter? On the demand side, Indian firms often complain that there is inadequate demand for their products. Yet, the world market in merchandise exports at USD 16.6 trillion in 2015 is extremely large. Why are Indian firms not able to take advantage of this massive demand? The likely explanation is that their products are not competitive in the global economy. The flip side of this point is that the discipline of the global economy is what leads to fast productivity growth. Exporters must compete against the best in the world and must therefore constantly upgrade technology, management and product quality to remain competitive.

In addition, the large size of the export market allows exporters to leverage scale economies. Many super-competitive firms operating in China today employ not just tens of thousands of workers but hundreds of thousands of them. These large firms create an ecosystem that enforces discipline and high productivity on smaller firms as well. In contrast, there are hardly any firms in India employing hundreds of thousands of workers. The apparel industry offers the starkest example: more than 90 percent of apparel workers in India were employed in firms with less than 50 workers in

2005. The corresponding figure in China was less than 15 percent the same year.

The importance of exports for the creation of jobs at decent wages should be clear. Exporting firms must maintain high productivity, which translates in high wages for their employees. Non-exporting firms either become ancillaries of the exporting firms or must compete against them in the domestic market. In either case, they must achieve high productivity to survive, which allows them to pay competitive wages. Recognizing this critical role of exports in the creation of well-paying jobs, India needs a focused strategy for creating an environment in which export competitive firms can emerge, especially in labour intensive sectors". [1]

While the trading environment is undeniably challenging, the confluence of several favourable factors gives India an unprecedented window of opportunity to set its house in order and face the challenges thrown up by an ever changing global economic environment. India's export sector is yet to take off in terms of share in world exports, though it has had bouts of high growth at different stretches of time. Some important issues in this sector are the following.

12.1 Credit Flow to Export Sector

In view of the importance of export credit in maintaining the pace of export growth, the RBI has, over the years, undertaken several measures to ensure timely and hassle-free flow of credit to the export sector. Banks extend working capital loans to exporters at pre- and post-shipment stages and the credit limits sanctioned to exporters are based upon the financing bank's perception of the creditworthiness and past performance of exporters. Export financing may be denominated either in Indian rupees or in foreign currency. For both types of pre-shipment (up to 180 days) and post-shipment (up to 90 days) financing, the RBI sets a ceiling on the interest rate that banks may charge to borrowers under the scheme. Since the RBI fixes only the ceiling rate of interest for export credit, banks are free to fix lower rates of interest for exporters on the basis of their actual cost of funds, operating expenses, the track record and the risk perception of the borrower/exporter.

In recent years, a number of measures have been undertaken by the RBI with a view to aligning the export credit schemes in tune with the changing environment. These measures, *inter alia*, have included the following.

1. Rationalisation and liberalisation of export credit interest rates.
2. Flexibility in repayment/prepayment of pre-shipment credit.
3. Special financial package for large value exporters.
4. Export finance for agricultural exports.
5. Freedom to banks to source funds from abroad without any limit exclusively for the purpose of granting export credit in foreign currency.

Following the proposal of the Ministry of Commerce and Industry in the Exim Policy 2003-04 released in January 2004, a Gold Card Scheme was drawn up by the RBI in May 2004 in consultation with select banks and exporters with a view to further simplifying access to bank credit by exporters, especially small and medium exporters and making it borrower-friendly in terms of procedure and credit terms. With effect from March 4, 2005, it was decided that the Scheme would not be applicable to those exporters who are blacklisted by the Export Credit Guarantee Corporation (ECGC) or included in the RBI's defaulter's list/caution list or making losses for the past three years or having overdue export bills in excess of 10 percent of the previous year's turnover.

12.1.1 Working Group to Review Export Credit, 2005: This Working Group (Chairman: Anand Sinha) was constituted with an overall objective to review the following.

1. Existing procedures for export credit.
2. Action taken on exporters' satisfaction survey.
3. Gold Card Scheme.

4. Export credit for non-star exporters.
5. Current interest rate structure in export credit.

The Working Group, on examination of the various aspects relating to its terms of reference, made a host of recommendations in its Report submitted in May 2005 to improve the existing export credit delivery mechanism.

The major recommendations of the Group are set out below:

1. Although existing procedures for export credit in place were adequate to take care of the interest of the exporters, there is a need for attitudinal change in approach of banks' officials. While posting officials, banks may keep in view the attitude of officials to exporters' credit requirements, especially the small and medium exporters.
2. Banks should post nodal officers at regional/zonal offices and major branches having substantial export credit for attending to the credit related problems of SME exporters.
3. Banks should put in place a control and reporting mechanism to ensure that the applications for export credit, especially from SMEs are disposed off within the prescribed timeframe.
4. Banks should raise all queries in one shot and should avoid piecemeal queries in order to avoid delays in sanctioning credit.
5. Allocation to collateral securities should be sound and fully made use of.
6. There was a need to look into the grievances of the small and medium exporters and a fresh "satisfaction survey" may be undertaken by an external agency regarding the satisfaction of the exporters with the services rendered by banks.
7. Since the number of Gold Cards issued by banks is small, banks may be advised to speed up the process and adopt a simplified procedure regarding issue of the Cards.
8. The Cards should be extended to all the eligible exporters, especially the SME exporters and the process may be completed within three months.

9. The present interest rate prescription by the RBI may continue for the time being in the interests of the small and medium exporters.
10. Interest rates on export credit in foreign currency may be raised by 25 basis points (i.e. LIBOR + 1 percent for the first slab and additional 2 percent for the second slab), subject to the express condition that the banks will not levy any other charges in any manner under any name *viz.* service charge, management charge etc. except for recovery towards out of pocket expenses incurred.
11. Banks should give priority for the foreign currency export credit requirements of exporters over foreign currency loans to non-exporter borrowers.
12. In view of the substantial increase in export credit in foreign currency through borrowings from abroad, there is a need to look into whether a regulatory limit could be prescribed, up to which banks may be allowed to borrow from abroad for the purpose.

12.2 Competitiveness of Exports

Exports of a country are deemed to be competitive if the country is able to sell its products at a lower or same price and earn the same return as its competitors. Export competitiveness of a country is determined by the following factors.

1. Favourable endowment base in the economy.
2. Transaction costs.
3. Better quality of the commodity produced.
4. Remuneration of factors of production.
5. Exchange rate.
6. Productivity through the use of better technical skills and human resource development.
7. Economies of scale.
8. Institutional and policy mechanisms.

Trade-related transaction costs are one of the major determinants of export competitiveness of an economy. Trade-related transaction costs refer to: (a) a large number of regulatory requirements, (b) compliance measures, (c) procedures and infrastructure-related costs (including communication costs with clients), (d) domestic transport costs to bring goods from the production site to the border, (e) time and money spent in ports on border procedures or to make products ready for shipment, (f) international transport costs and (g) inspection and certification costs.

Analysis of competitiveness of manufactured exports, as measured by a menu of indicators, reveals that India has comparative advantage with respect to some key indicators, *viz.* real exchange rate, labour productivity and unit labour cost. In fact, the unit labour cost of manufacturing exports in India is one of the lowest among the developing countries.

In their cost structure and productivity the principal industries, specially the export industries, must become competitive as early as possible, and a systematic programme to this end has to be pursued within each industry. This is an essential condition for diversifying exports and for steadily increasing the share of new manufacturers in the export trade. It is true that over a significant range of products Indian industry is capable of competing in export markets or, at any rate, of becoming reasonably competitive. However, the range of these industries is not large enough at present.

Studies show that vis-à-vis products exported by some of the major East Asian countries, Indian products have been losing their competitiveness. This has been attributed to mainly two kinds of reasons. The first kind relates to the state of infrastructure, factor policies, ease of doing business, facilitation at the borders and the system of taxation.

The other reasons are that: (a) India is relatively less integrated into regional and global supply chains, (b) existing trade architecture has not been used to its full potential and (c) there is relatively less focus on value-added exports and consequently marketing arrangements for positioning Indian products at higher levels of value realisation are inadequate. Interventions are needed to address many of these inadequacies.

12.3 Medium Term Export Strategy (MTES)

The Tenth Five Year Plan (2002-07) projected a growth rate of 12.4 percent in exports. The roadmap for the achievement of this export growth in the medium-term was delineated in the Medium Term Export Strategy (MTES), which was aimed at augmenting the country's share in world trade to 1 percent by 2006-07 from the then existing 0.7 percent which implied doubling exports from the existing level. The MTES also took into account the international developments and the complexities arising in the new world trade order under the WTO. A number of key macro policy issues for the commodities sector were discussed in the MTES, such as price competitiveness, implementation of trade defence mechanisms, efficient administration of tax rebate schemes, and conclusion of strategic free trade agreements.

The MTES incorporated product and market identification for exports as well as focus on sector-wise micro and macro strategies for identifying potential sectors based on the assessment of the changing global trade scenario and real and revealed comparative advantages. The strategy made an opportunity assessment after examining the import basket of major importing economies of the world and identifying potential items of exports in which India is competitive vis-à-vis some of the major exporting countries of these products.

Some of the sectors emphasised included the following: engineering, electronic, electrical and allied sectors, textiles sector, gems and jewellery, chemicals and allied sectors, agriculture and allied sectors, leather and leather manufactures. An institutional mechanism was set up to monitor the implementation of the strategy.

12.4 Restraining Domestic Consumption

Domestic consumption must be held within reasonable limits with a view to creating the surpluses for exports. Restraints on the growth of internal consumption are an essential condition of a successful export drive. They have to be resorted to where supplies are insufficient for meeting both home and foreign demands. They have also to be adopted where supplies could be increased through larger investments so as to save on internal resources as well as foreign exchange. As a rule, what is required is not absolute reduction in the total or the per capita consumption but only a slowing down in the rate at which consumption increases. In taking these and other measures it is of course essential that there should be greater public understanding of the need to step up exports and recognition that this object cannot be achieved without a degree of sacrifice which is equitably shared.

For achieving the export objectives, it is necessary not only to create the surpluses for exports, but also to ensure that the surpluses become available at prices competitive with those of other suppliers in markets abroad. Competitive export capacity depends largely on internal prices. From this point of view it is vital that inflationary pressures associated with development should be held in check.

Steps must be taken to mobilise public opinion in favour of exports and acceptance of the burdens involved, to enlist the cooperation of industry and trade in this national effort, to improve Government's own organisation for market research and intelligence and commercial representation abroad, and to enlarge facilities for credit, insurance etc.

12.5 Product Diversification

While there has been market diversification and compositional changes in India's export basket, not much of demand-based product diversification has taken place. Most of the items in the top 100 world imports include the three Es—electronic, electrical, and engineering items—and some textiles items. Though the gain in shares of engineering goods in recent years is a positive sign, India lags behind many other competing countries. Special attention needs to be given to the electronics hardware sector which virtually collapsed with the signing of the Information Technology Agreement (ITA)-1 by

India at a time when India's semiconductor sector was at a nascent stage of development, while that of newly industrialized countries (NICs) and developed countries had already taken off. Till now, India's focus was on exporting what it can (or supply based), now it has to shift to items for which there is world demand and India also has basic competence. A demand-based export basket diversification approach with a perceptible shift to the three Es could lead to greater dividends for India.

Based on domestic manufacturing capabilities and potential demand, exports of drugs and pharmaceuticals, chemicals and the electronic sector (all high value products reliant on manufacturing base) would need to grow significantly to realize the overall growth targets. Another important category that needs to grow is that of exports based on light manufacturing sectors, i.e. leather products and textiles. These are important because they generate employment, have high domestic value addition, and have historically been areas of strength in India's export markets. In leather, the product basket must be diversified. Instead of exporting finished leather, India must move into value-added products, especially high-end shoes and leather garments. In textiles, India needs to realize more effectively the scope for growth made possible since the dismantling of the quota regime. Product diversification in garments is essential. India must focus on women's garments, value added cotton products, and a large thrust on synthetic textiles. In both these sectors, scaling up operations and increasing export growth rates should be aimed at.

12.6 Export Infrastructure

Leaving aside the external environment, infrastructure bottlenecks are the most critical constraints to achieving accelerated export growth. There are two categories of infrastructure requirements:

1. Better multi-modal transportation for improved road

connectivity to ports, rail heads and airports, faster throughput at ports and shorter dwell time, faster movement of rakes by railways and quicker air cargo movement with all the concomitant trade facilitation measures in place.

2. Supportive infrastructure required for exports including more laboratories for testing, more tool rooms and plant quarantine facilities, larger trade facilitation centres and land customs stations and enhanced cold storage facilities for pharmaceutical and perishable goods.

Export infrastructure, particularly ports-related infrastructure, which affects trade, needs immediate attention. Even the best of India's ports do not have state-of-the-art technology as in Singapore, Rotterdam, and Shanghai. Port infrastructure issues include poor road conditions and port connectivity, congestions, vessel berthing delays, poor cargo handling techniques and equipment, and lack of access for containerized cargo, resulting in multiple handlings, increased lead time, high transaction costs, and thus loss of market competitiveness. Export infrastructure should be built on a war footing. Just as drastic changes have been brought about in India's airports and metro rail, sea ports should be the immediate priority.

12.7 Export Promotion Schemes

There are multiple and overlapping export promotion schemes with many focus markets and focus products with items and markets getting added each year in the foreign trade policy. One thing that is visible even from the short select list of trade policy measures is the multiplicity of schemes and concessions that are also periodically extended. There is need to rationalize the export promotion schemes to a bare minimum which can also reduce transaction costs and trade litigations. Also many rates of concession should not be there. Even for duty drawback schemes, there should be limited rates instead of having different rates even for similar items. This will make things simpler and avoid discretionary decisions.

Wherever tariffs are low or can be reduced, export incentives should be withdrawn as the transaction costs would be higher than the benefits owing to duty concessions.

12.7.1 Market Access Initiative (MAI) and Market Development Assistance (MDA) Schemes: MAI scheme is an umbrella instrument for supporting trade promotion initiatives. The scheme, which was launched in 2003, has been revised from time to time. The activities which are supported under the scheme broadly include the organization of exhibitions, buyer seller meets, seminars, conferences and conventions; supporting participation in established exhibitions; supporting brochures, catalogues and other such literature; supporting registration and specific requirements in some sectors such as the pharmaceutical sector; and supporting studies with the specific objective of facilitating a better understanding of commodities and markets.

Under the MDA Scheme, financial assistance is provided for a range of export promotion activities implemented by Export Promotion Councils and Trade Promotion Organizations.

12.8 Trade Facilitation

The smooth flow of goods and services across borders is one of the most significant elements contributing to a country's competitiveness at the global level. In India there are bottlenecks at two levels. Firstly, the movement of goods within the country, from one territory to another, is constrained by the laws, practices, regulations and taxation regimes of various States. The second bottleneck is caused by infrastructure constraints at the border, such as the lack of necessary equipment and testing facilities at the border ports, human resource inadequacies etc., resulting in port and road congestion.

Action in respect of many of these issues lies with several departments of the Government of India such as the Ministry of Shipping, Ministry of Agriculture, Ministry of Finance, Ministry of Road Transport and the State Governments.

Concerted action is, therefore, the need of the hour.

In recognition of the fact that export promotion efforts through schemes and stimulus packages will be ineffective unless transaction costs are substantially lowered, the Government has taken a number of initiatives over the years to streamline export/import processes and facilitate trade and industry so as to make doing business in India easier. High transaction costs directly impact the competitiveness of Indian exporters vis-à-vis exporters of competing countries.

Greater trade facilitation by removing the delays and high costs on account of procedural and documentation factors, besides infrastructure bottlenecks is another major challenge. As per the World Bank and International Finance Corporation (IFC) publication Doing Business 2014, India ranks 134 in ease of doing business with Singapore at first place and China at 96. In trading across borders India ranks 132, Singapore 1, and China 74. India needs 9 export documents compared to 3 in Singapore and 8 in China. Time to export is 16 days in India and 6 in Singapore. The number of import documents needed is 20 for India and 4 for Singapore. Cost of exports per container is US$ 1170 in India, US$ 460 in Singapore, and US$ 620 in China and cost of imports per container is US$ 1250 in India, US$ 440 in Singapore, and US$ 615 in China. There are also inter-ministerial delays. The present move towards integration of related ministries is a step in the right direction, though a lot more needs to be done.

12.9 Adhering to Standards and Building India Brand

There is a synergistic relationship between standards and trade. Adherence to standards enhances the potential of trade because standards reduce information asymmetry, signal quality to consumers and create a common language for potential trading partners, thus reducing overall transaction costs. At the same time the concerns about standards acting as non-tariff barriers (NTBs) in global trade are also well-documented.

It is essential for India to develop a coordinated national response and strategy to meet the challenges of standards and conformity assessment and promote its presence in the international market.

Presently, nations, businesses and people are competing for the same global share of trade, investment, business and tourism in the backdrop of a rapidly changing global context, fragile global economic recovery and newer and faster technologies. Many countries are allocating huge resources for brand promotion.

A long term branding strategy is required for India to hold its own in this highly competitive environment, not merely to attract consumers but, more importantly, to encourage industry to position its products in highly discerning markets and to ensure that Brand India becomes synonymous with high quality.

Brands fetch additional value for their promoters. They also bring additional institutional recognition to the country because building a brand is a long term comprehensive procedure in which several stakeholders play a role. Therefore, the capacity of a local brand to acquire global recognition needs to be rewarded. It is a difficult exercise but in the backdrop of the conceptual development of Brand India, a logical follow up should be to promote those brands which have the potential to be or which have already become global brands.

12.10 Digitisation and E-governance

For export-import operations, the costs involved, as well as the complexity of the documents and the procedures, are a major burden for business. For small and medium-sized companies, especially, these costs act as a major disincentive to engage in international trade. Since goods cannot travel faster than the information that controls them, speeding up the information exchange makes trading more competitive and efficient.

All operations related to exports and imports should be automated and paperless. A firm should be able to submit all information required by government and related agencies through a single window. South Korea, Singapore and many other countries have implemented such systems. An integrated single window, through which smooth and speedy clearance can be enabled without compromising on compliance, is the need of the hour.

Government has already launched a very ambitious programme for digitization under its Digital India initiative. Under the National e-governance programme, subsumed within the Digital India initiative, the e-Trade programme has a strong focus area with the objective of ensuring transparency, simplification and faster action.

12.11 Future of India's Exports

In the Indian context, exports are still seen to be primarily supply-side determined. Although demand-related factors, like relative prices (including exchange-rate movements) and world incomes, are becoming progressively more important, particularly for specific export items, the dominant factor continues to be the ability of the economy to produce adequate volumes of exportables to address international markets.

Fish products, other food and beverages, textiles, readymade garments, other non-metallic minerals (including pearls, precious and semi-precious stones), leather products, petroleum products, chemicals, iron and steel, machinery and communication and electronic items are expected to constitute the highest share of exports.

Government has recognized that higher growth cannot take place without tapping the opportunities offered by the global economy in terms of markets, investment and technologies along with improvement in efficiency and absorbing excess capacity available in the economy. An important pre-condition for establishing a more open economy is to create an expanding production base of tradable goods and services, which will not only withstand external competition, but also provide the surplus necessary to ensure sufficient export earnings for meeting the import needs of the country.

Another pre-condition is to create an environment under which the export market becomes increasingly more attractive, so that there is both a shift from selling in the domestic market to exports and developing capacities to specifically target such export opportunities. Re-orientation of the incentive structure towards investment in tradable goods and services and away from non-tradables combined with improvement in relative profitability of exports vis-à-vis domestic sales would lead to higher production for exports.

Even if the labour cost of producing a unit of manufacturing exports in India is one of the lowest among the developing countries, labour market rigidity is perceived as a major operating constraint. For boosting foreign investment infusion, labour policies will have to be made more flexible. There is a need for a radical strategy to promote services exports in which India has a competitive advantage.

It has been observed that in contrast to the structural and compositional shifts in world trade towards higher technology-intensive products, the commodity structure of India's exports remained largely unchanged until the mid-1990s. Although, of late, India's exports have shown a steady trend towards higher technology content, India's specialisation in exports lies in manufactures based on labour and natural resources essentially involving low technology. Given the export structure of India, the potential for further growth of manufactured goods, especially to the developed markets remains high. However, given the general trend of movement of terms of trade towards higher technology-intensive products, it may be imperative for India to move up the technology ladder.

To sum up, aggressively promoting export growth of high value products that have a strong domestic manufacturing base is the lynchpin of overall export growth strategy. Most important in this category are exports of engineering goods. Increasing exports of engineering goods has to be a major goal in any strategy to increase exports.

Rapidly changing technology requires the country to adapt production and export strategies to provide products that meet consumer/producer demands in India's exporting markets. To establish greater credibility and acceptance of India's critical export products and sectors in foreign markets, it is necessary to strengthen efforts to build up a brand image for important Indian exports, and promote a thrust for quality upgradation. Domestic standards for export related products should be raised, assurances put in place of quality enforcement through appropriate agencies, and expanded certification of export products encouraged, where needed.

Unlike the East Asian countries where industry has been the major driver of exports growth, the contribution of industrial exports in India has been comparatively low. This could perhaps be attributed to small-scale industry reservations and inflexible labour laws besides infrastructural bottlenecks. The labour cost in India, however, is one of the lowest among its competitor countries. Given the exports structure of India, the potential for higher exports of manufactures, especially to the developed countries, is high.

India's export competitiveness is being challenged not only by China and South-East Asian countries but also by newly emerging Asian countries like Bangladesh, and Vietnam in items like textiles. The challenge for India is to achieve a share in world trade commensurate with its size. Despite making great strides in its export growth, India has not made much progress in terms of the share in world trade. India's exports were higher than those of China till 1954. In 2010, the shares of China and India in world exports stood at 10.5 percent and 1.5 percent respectively. If India can attain at least half of China's share in world exports, the impact on its employment and manufacturing activity will be enormous. While trade policy measures, shift in focus to some markets and some products, trade facilitation, tariff reforms etc. have helped in some measure, if India has to achieve a substantial share in world exports, a big push will be needed.

While India has diversified its export basket as well as export markets over the years, substantial diversification in tune with world demand has not taken place. There are many electronic, electrical, and engineering items where India's presence is negligible. For the future, the prospects of sustained growth in exports of goods and services are bright provided the Indian economy can face the challenge of enhancing productivity and competitiveness in an increasingly integrated global environment.

To boost exports, supportive measures are necessary as is adequate infrastructure. Simultaneously, concerted efforts need to be directed at creating domestic capacity in production of goods where India's import dependency is high and increasing.

Trade remedies are a legitimate method of addressing unfair trade practices. While India is a strong votary of free trade and benefits from it, yet it has used trade remedial measures where required and will continue to do so if unfair practices are adopted by trading partners or their business entities.

Endnote

1. NITI Aayog, *India: Three Year Action Agenda (2017-18 to 2019-20)*, August 2017, p. 34.

13

Composition and Origin of Imports

13.1 Euphoria for Import Substitution

The rapid depletion of the sterling balances soon after Independence forced the Government of India to follow a restrictive import policy. Broadly speaking, that policy consisted of dividing imports into three categories: (a) free, (b) restricted and (c) prohibited. Imports of food, capital goods, the raw materials of industry and certain essential consumer goods were free and no exchange restrictions were placed upon their import. Consumer goods which were not absolutely essential were licensed on a quota basis, while others which in the context of the economy of India were regarded as totally unessential and luxury imports were altogether prohibited.

India adopted an inward-looking development strategy after independence wherein import substitution constituted a major element of both trade and industrial policies. Import substitution was the prime objective of India's trade policy till the mid-1970s. This policy was largely based on the Imports and Exports (Control) Act of 1947 and the Import Trade Control Order of 1955. Import substitution was significant in the area of industrial machinery, paper, chemicals, iron and steel and non-ferrous metals.

13.2 Reduction in Tariff and Non-tariff Barriers

A key aspect of the trade reforms of the 1990s was the reduction in import duties. The broad approach to reforms regarding customs tariffs and exemptions was laid out in the Report of Tax Reforms Committee, 1991 (Chairman: Raja Chelliah). India's customs tariff rates have been declining since 1991. The peak rate came down progressively from 150 percent in 1991-92 to 25 percent in 2003-04. Effective January

9, 2004, the peak rate of customs duty on non-agricultural goods was further reduced to 20 percent. After successive downward revisions, the peak rate of duty for the financial year 2012-13 is 10 percent.

The fall in peak duty has not led to the feared collapse in revenue collections. The duty cuts have neither wiped out the domestic manufacturing sector nor resulted in large-scale unemployment as predicted by many. The data show that successive peak duty cuts have been accompanied by rise in customs duty collections. However, further bold tariff reforms with minimum revenue loss are needed to reach levels comparable to those in ASEAN both for peak rate as well as total duty.

Non-tariff barriers are generally considered less desirable than tariffs. The most common non-tariff barriers are the restrictions or prohibitions on imports maintained through the import licensing requirements. In the Indian context, for several decades quantitative restrictions (QRs) on imports of a wide range of products (mainly consumer goods) were justified for balance of payments reasons. With the external sector gathering strength, along with reduction in tariffs, India has been following a policy for gradual removal of restriction on imports since 1991.

There has been a steady decline in both nominal and effective rates of protection. Although there has been a significant decline in average tariff rates, the dispersion of tariff has not declined enough. Unlike major tariff liberalisation initiatives in East Asian and Latin American countries due to regional trade agreements, trade liberalisation in India has mainly been the result of its own unilateral initiative rather than brought about by multilateral trade commitments or regional trade agreements. In fact, in most items, India's customs tariff rates are at present significantly lower than the corresponding *bound* rates stemming from obligations undertaken in the WTO.

13.3 Composition of Imports

The structure of India's imports has undergone changes since the opening up of the Indian economy. With the move away from import substitution and towards promotion of trade based on dynamic advantage, the policy distinction between essential imports and otherwise has gradually subsided. Commodity-wise analysis reveals that while petroleum still continues to have a dominant presence in India's imports, capital goods and other intermediary products for export purposes have emerged as key items of imports.

There have been a number of subtle compositional shifts within the broad level of aggregation in recent years. For instance, within the petroleum imports, there has been a shift from import of petroleum products towards crude imports following a large scale increase of refinery capacity over time. Furthermore, India has transformed itself from a net importer of finished petroleum products to net exporter of the same.

Another significant development has been the channellising of imports of gold through officially designated routes. Since 1997 when banks were allowed to import gold, the import of gold through passenger baggage has declined significantly.

Furthermore, in the recent past the share of bulk items has increased while that of non-bulk items has declined. Amongst the bulk items, share of POL has increased rather sharply. The share of bulk consumption goods in imports, mainly comprising food items, has been fluctuating according to domestic demand. Share in import of other bulk items like rubber, pulp and paper, wood and wood products, fertilizers, metallic-ferrous ores and metal scrap, non-ferrous metals, and iron and steel decreased till 2000-01, although it increased thereafter. Share of capital goods has shown a consistent declining trend.

Share of export related items consisting of chemicals, pearls and precious stones, cashew, textile yarn and fabric, leather, raw cotton, silk, wool and jute has remained steady in the recent past.

13.3.1 Gems and Jewellery: Rough diamonds are mostly imported by India. With pro-active involvement of the Government in the Kimberley Process and continuous follow up within the framework of the existing bilateral institutional mechanisms, Indian industry could source roughs directly from Russia, Namibia and Zimbabwe. These efforts need to be pursued with greater momentum and an aggressive policy needs to be developed to ensure continuous supply of roughs from these countries. Similarly, there is a need to explore continuous supply of coloured gemstones from countries like Brazil, Russia, Tanzania, and Myanmar.

Gem and jewellery industry is an import-based industry which requires foreign currency, i.e. US Dollars. To ensure easy and continuous availability of roughs from overseas mining companies and for its marketing and infrastructure needs, there is a need to ensure bank finance in foreign currency at international interest rates and costs.

It is necessary to allow consignment import of rough diamonds. Under this system both the cut and polished, and rough diamonds are imported on consignment basis from across the world and are assorted in different lots according to the cut and polished size and displayed for auction. After the bidding, diamonds are taken by the bidder and the unsold diamonds are re-exported back.

The composition of India's imports in 2018-19 is shown in Table 13.1.

13.4 Import Intensity of Exports in India

Import intensity of exports can simply be defined as the degree of value addition of an imported item that subsequently gets exported. In the Indian context, gems and jewellery is a typical example of such export product having high import intensity. Another way of defining import intensity of exports is to identify those exports which are heavily dependent on imported inputs. These imported inputs may belong to the same sector or a different sector altogether.

Table 13.1: Commodity Composition of India's Imports: 2018-19

(Descending order)

S. No.	Commodity	US$ million
1.	Petroleum crude and products	1,40,918
2.	Electronic goods	55,471
3.	Machinery, electrical and non-electrical	39,760
4.	Gold	32,897
5.	Pearls, precious and semi-precious stones	27,076
6.	Coal, coke and briquettes etc.	26,172
7.	Transport equipment	24,760
8.	Organic and inorganic chemicals	23,828
9.	Iron and steel	17,656
10.	Artificial resins, plastic materials etc.	15,681
11.	Non-ferrous metals	14,733
12.	Vegetable oils	9,890
13.	Chemical material and products	7,708
14.	Metaliferrous ores and other minerals	7,581
15.	Fertilizers, crude and manufactures	7,467
16.	Medicinal and pharmaceutical products	6,359
17.	Wood and wood products	6,126
18.	Professional instruments, optical goods etc.	5,187
19.	Machine tools	4,642
20.	Silver	3,748
21.	Dyeing, tanning, colouring materials	3,222
22.	Project goods	2,306
23.	Fruits and vegetables	2,144
24.	Textile yarn, fabrics and made-ups	1,900
25.	Pulp and waste paper	1,312
26.	Pulses	1,141
27.	Leather and leather products	1,058
28.	Newsprint	978
29.	Cotton raw and waste	633
30.	Sulphur and unroasted iron pyrts	217
31.	Other commodities	21,391
32	Total imports	5,14,034

Note: Total may differ due to rounding off of individual items.

Source: Reserve Bank of India, *Handbook of Statistics on Indian Economy, 2018-19*, Table 122; data rearranged.

Imports may not only have a direct impact on exports through the import content but may also have an indirect effect in augmenting exports through other indirect spill over channels. Thus, a broader definition of import intensity of exports incorporates not only the direct quantum of imports that is channelled to exports but also the indirect effects of imported products that augment exports.

A select set of items could be identified that are mainly imported for export purposes, such as gems and jewellery, chemicals and allied products, textile yarn and fabrics. A comparison of corresponding finished products that are exported by value-adding these import items show high import intensity in gems and jewellery and chemicals and allied products. The extent of such import intensity, however, appears to be declining for both the items since the early 1990s.

In this context, it is interesting to note that despite significant liberalisation of imports—reduction in tariffs, phasing out of QRs and allowing official bullion imports—the country's current account deficit has remained modest during the 1990s. Furthermore, the overall balance of payments has been in surplus in recent years and the country's foreign exchange reserves in terms of import cover have improved significantly. Thus, in contrast to fears expressed at the time of the economy's opening up, import liberalisation policies, in conjunction with overall structural reforms, have considerably strengthened the country's external sector and contributed to overall development since 1990-91.

13.5 Origin of Imports

Prior to Independence, India's trade relations were confined mainly to Britain and other Commonwealth countries. Over the last 65 years significant changes have taken place in India's direction of exports and sources of imports.

Subsequent to the opening up, India's imports are being

sourced from a wider range of countries. Traditionally important trading partners like Germany, Japan, UK and Australia have subsided in terms of their market share and new import partners from Africa and East Asia (including China) have emerged and are increasingly gaining importance. In recent years, Belgium, from where India imports its major export-oriented item of gems and jewellery, has emerged as one of the principal sources of imports.

Another interesting feature has been the gradual dissipation of the Commonwealth of Independent States (CIS) countries as major sources of India's imports. Furthermore, the OECD countries, and EU in particular, have been the major supplier of the import items. The share of imports from OPEC and Russia has declined while the share of imports from Africa, Asia and Latin America has remained more or less constant. Table 13.2 shows the origin of India's imports by country groups and countries for the year 2018-19.

Table 13.2: Origin of India's Imports: 2018-19

Country Group	**US$ million**
I. OECD countries, of which	1,44,865
A. European Union, of which	58,434
a. France	6,666
b. Germany	15,161
c. UK	7,562
B. North America, of which	39,065
a. Canada	3,515
b. USA	35,549
C. Asia and Oceania, of which	26,535
a. Australia	13,131
b. Japan	12,772
D. Other OECD countries, of which	20,831
a. Switzerland	18,077
II. OPEC countries, of which	1,36,546
a. Iran	13,526

contd...

b. Iraq	22,372
c. Kuwait	7,431
d. Saudi Arabia	28,479
e. UAE	29,783
III. Eastern Europe, of which	9,466
a. Russia	5,840
IV. Developing countries, of which	2,23,010
A. Asia, of which	1,79,875
a. China	70,319
b. South Korea	16,759
c. Singapore	16,282
B. Africa	24,449
C. Latin America	18,686
V. Others	58
VI. Unspecified	89
Total Imports	5,14,034

Source: Reserve Bank of India, *Handbook of Statistics on Indian Economy, 2018-19*, Table 134.

13.6 Agricultural Imports

In recent years, edible oil, accounting for nearly 60 to 65 percent of the value of total agriculture imports, has become the single largest import item. Raw cashew, nuts (almonds from US) and pulses are among the other dominant agriculture imports. Of late, the share of agriculture imports in total imports of the country has hovered around 4 to 5 percent.

13.6.1 Protecting Domestic Agriculture: Lifting of quantitative restrictions on imports since April 2000 has resulted in import of a number of agriculture products which include fruits, juices, ketchups, meat products etc. Monitoring of 300 sensitive product imports has so far revealed that such imports are limited and, in the aggregate, constitute a small proportion of total agriculture imports. Contrary to concerns in some circles that liberalization of imports—resulting from the lifting of quantitative restrictions on agriculture products—would lead to surge of agriculture imports affecting adversely the Indian farmers, the value of agriculture imports in aggregate terms is quite low. India has considerable flexibility to counter flooding of the Indian market by cheap agriculture imports through imposition of tariffs (bound rate) under WTO. WTO permissible tariff rates are reasonably high as compared to actual rates. This should provide a fair level of protection. Countervailing duties can also be imposed to counter questionable subsidies given to agriculture products by the exporting countries apart from having the option of acting under safeguard provisions to counter surge of imports.

A Joint Working Group on Agriculture and Marine Products has been set up for facilitating and promoting agricultural trade between India and European Union. The 4th meeting of the Joint Working Group was held in Brussels on May 28, 2010 to discuss agricultural policies, growth in bilateral trade and issues of mutual interest related to agricultural trade.

To sum up, despite some initial apprehensions, liberalisation has not adversely affected India's balance of payments. On the contrary, increased trade liberalisation along with prudent management of capital account liberalisation has imparted significant strength to the balance of payments since the mid-1990s. Thus, in contrast to fears expressed at the time of the opening up of the economy, import liberalisation policies have, in fact, strengthened the country's external sector. The implication is that continued reduction in import tariffs will help in inducing greater efficiency and competitiveness in the economy, while reducing avoidable transaction costs in trade.

With the increased competitiveness of Indian industry, imports of low and medium-technology intensive products have declined. At the same time, imports of high-technology intensive products and imports used for export production have increased. There is growing evidence that accessibility to imports has a positive impact on the growth performance of the country. The behaviour of aggregate import demand in the country is expected to be strongly driven by domestic growth rates.

India has large agricultural imports both in terms of pulses, edible oils and other commodities. An aggressive policy reform package with medium-term objectives to increase yields and domestic production needs to be put in place immediately. There is need to rationalise fertilizer pricing and production policy to encourage efficiency in use, consumption and production so that dependence on imports is reduced.

Electronic machinery and electronic goods imports will increase unless India establishes a domestic fabrication facility and dramatically expand domestic production of these items. Priority attention is necessary if the huge growth in imports on this account is to be checked.

14

Customs Duties

14.1 Legislative Framework

The Constitution of India grants exclusive powers to the Central Government to impose duties of customs. By virtue of entry 83 of List I (Union List) in the Seventh Schedule of the Constitution of India, the Central Government is empowered to impose 'duties of customs including export duties'.

During the British rule, various customs and tariff enactments were passed from time to time, the following two being the main: (a) The Sea Customs Act, 1878, and (b) The Tariff Act, 1934.

After Independence, the Sea Customs Act, 1878 and other allied enactments (Inland Bounded Warehousing Act, 1896 and the Land Customs Act, 1924) were repealed by a consolidating and amending legislation entitled the Customs Act, 1962. Similarly, the Tariff Act of 1934 was repealed by the Customs Tariff Act, 1975.

14.2 Customs Act, 1962

This is the main Act which provides, vide section 12, for the levy and collection of customs duty. This power is derived by virtue of entry 83 of List I (Union List) in the Seventh Schedule of the Constitution of India. Besides, the Act provides import/export procedures, prohibition on importation and exportation of goods, offences penalties etc. It stands as a complete code in itself as to the levy and collection of duties on import and export of goods.

14.2.1 Rules under Customs Act, 1962: Section 156 of Customs Act empowers the Central Government to make rules, consistent with provisions of the Act, to carry out the purposes of the Act. Thus, the Government has framed various rules some of which are as under:

1. Customs Valuation (Determination of Value of Imported Goods) Rules, 2007.
2. Customs Valuation (Determination of Value of Export Goods) Rules, 2007.
3. Baggage Rules, 1998.

14.2.2 Regulations under Customs Act, 1962: Under section 157 of the Customs Act, the Central Board of Indirect Taxes and Customs (CBIC) [Earlier Central Board of Excise and Customs (CBEC)] is empowered to make regulations, consistent with the provisions of the Act, to carry out the purposes of the Act. Different regulations have been framed within the parameters of these powers as, for example, Project Import Regulations, 1986.

Similarly, CBIC can issue circulars, instructions, directions for the purpose of uniformity in classification of goods and with respect to the levy of duty thereon.

14.3 Customs Tariff Act, 1975

It contains two schedules. Schedule 1 includes various import items in systematic categories—in accordance with the international scheme of classification of internationally-traded goods known as Harmonized System of Commodity Classification—and specifies the rate of import duties thereon, as prescribed by the legislature. Schedule 2 incorporates items that are subject to export duties and the rate of duties thereon. Further, it makes provisions for additional duty (CVD), preferential duty, anti-dumping duty, protective duties etc.

Customs duties are generally levied either on specific or *ad valorem* basis, but in some cases specific-cum-ad valorem duties are also levied.

14.4 Various Types of Customs Duties

In accordance with the provisions of the Constitution, various types of customs duties are imposed by the Government under different Acts of Parliament.

Goods become liable to import duty when there is *import into* India. Import is completed only when goods cross the customs barrier. This crossing of customs barrier is the taxable event in the case of imports.

Goods become liable for export duty when there is *export from* India. Export is completed when goods cross territorial waters of India. [1] Although export duty is collected before the ship leaves the port, it does not mean that taxable event has taken place. One can say that export duty is collected in advance.

Following are the important customs duties levied on goods imported into or exported from India.

14.4.1 Basic Customs Duty (BCD): Under Section 12 of the Customs Act, 1962 (the main enactment), duty of customs is levied at such rates as may be specified under Customs Tariff Act, 1975 on goods imported into, or exported from India. This is known as basic customs duty (BCD). It is levied under Section 12 of the Customs Act and specified under Section 2 of the Customs Tariff Act.

As per Section 2 of the Customs Tariff Act, the rates at which duties of customs shall be levied are indicated in the First Schedule and the Second Schedule of this Act. First Schedule deals with import tariff and Second Schedule with export tariff.

The duty may be a percentage of the value of the goods or at a specific rate. The Central Government has the power to reduce or exempt any goods from these duties.

14.4.2 Integrated Goods and Services Tax (IGST): It is noteworthy that Goods and Services Tax (GST) was introduced in India with effect from July 1, 2017. IGST—as a part of GST regime—is levied on inter-State supply of goods and services. IGST also applies on imports.

All exports (whether of goods or services) as well as supplies to SEZs have been categorized as zero-rated supplies in the IGST Act.

14.4.3 Anti-dumping Duty: Dumping occurs when one

country (say China) exports an article to another country (say India) at a price lower than its normal value. Since this is an unfair trade practice having a disruptive effect on international trade, anti-dumping duty comes in handy as a measure to rectify the situation.

Thus, if an article is exported from outside India to India at less than its normal value, the Central Government can impose anti-dumping duty on such transaction. It can be imposed by issue of a notification under section 9A of the Customs Tariff Act, 1975. However, anti-dumping duty cannot exceed *margin of dumping* in relation to such article. Margin of dumping means the difference between *normal value* and *export price*. Normal value means comparable price in ordinary course in trade, for like article, when destined for consumption in the exporting country. Export price means the price at which goods are exported.

Anti-dumping duty is generally imposed in cases where Indian production units are manufacturing similar articles. [2]

It is noteworthy that Section 9B(1)(b) of Customs Tariff Act, 1975 provides restrictions on the power of the Government to impose anti-dumping duty in the case of imports from a WTO member country. In such cases, anti-dumping duty can be imposed only if the Central Government declares that import of such articles in India causes material injury to Industry established in India or materially retards the establishment of any industry in India.

14.4.4 Safeguard Duty: Central Government can impose safeguard duty under section 8B of the Customs Tariff Act, 1975. This duty can be imposed on specified imported goods if the Government is satisfied that the goods are being imported in such increased quantity and under such conditions that they are causing serious injury to the domestic industry. Safeguard duty is valid for 4 years. The period of 4 years can be extended but the aggregate period cannot be more than 10 years.

14.4.5 Protective Duty: It is a duty imposed on imported goods for protection of interests of any industry in India on the recommendation of Tariff Commission. As per Sections 6 and 7, protective duty is effective from the date specified in the First Schedule of the Customs Tariff Act, 1975.

14.4.6 Social Welfare Surcharge: It is levied at the rate of 10 percent of the aggregate duties of Customs, on imported goods, to help provide for social welfare schemes of the Government.

14.5 Exemptions from Customs Duty

Customs duty exemptions are provided through provisions of Customs Act, 1962 and Customs Tariff Act, 1975. Central Government can also grant exemptions by issuing a notification under Section 25 of the Customs Act. Exemptions given by notifications may be unconditional or subject to conditions given in the notification. Different exemption notifications have been issues for duty free imports by Ministry of Defence, Indian Navy, Coast Guards and other Central/State organizations.

General exemptions have been granted for imports by privileged organizations like United Nations agencies.

Endnotes

1. Territorial sea, as defined by the 1982 United Nations Convention on the Law of the Sea, is a belt of coastal waters extending at most 12 nautical miles (22.2 km.) from the baseline (usually the mean low-water mark) of a coastal state.
2. See also section 16.5 of chapter 16 of this book.

15

Imports and Goods and Services Tax (GST)

15.1 Meaning of Imports of Goods and Services

Import of goods means bringing goods into India from a place outside India. Import of services means the supply of any service where

- the supplier of service is located outside India;
- the recipient of service is located in India; and
- the place of supply of service is in India.

15.2 Imports are Inter-state Supplies

As per explanation to clause (1) of Article 269A of the Constitution, IGST (CGST plus SGST) will be levied on all imports into the territory of India. Thus, import of goods is treated as inter-state supplies and hence subject to IGST in addition to the applicable customs duties. Import of services is treated as inter-state supplies and hence subject to IGST.

15.3 Applicability of IGST

IGST is applicable by virtue of Section 3(7) of the Customs Tariff Act, 1975 which was amended with effect from July 1, 2017. The amended version provides that any article which is imported into India shall be liable to IGST at such rate which is leviable under Section 5 of IGST Act, 2017 on a like article on its supply in India.

Section 3(7) of the Customs Tariff Act, 1975 reads as follows, "any article which is imported into India shall, in addition, be liable to integrated tax at such rate, not exceeding forty percent, as is leviable under Section 5 of the Integrated Goods and Services Tax Act, 2017 on a like article on its supply in India, on the value of the imported article…".

Input tax credit pertaining to IGST paid is available on

import of goods and services. BCD paid on import is not eligible for set-off.

IGST rate is broadly equal to Central Goods and Services Tax (CGST) rate plus State Goods and Services Tax (SGST) rate. SGST component of IGST accrues to the consumer state. In other words, the incidence of tax follows the destination principle and the SGST component of tax revenue accrues to the state where the imported goods and services are consumed. Unlike in the past, the states where imported goods are consumed now gain their share from the IGST paid on imported goods.

15.4 Rationale for IGST on Imports

In order to understand the rationale for IGST on imports, it is necessary to know about basic customs duty (BCD).

Under Section 12 of the Customs Act, 1962 (the main enactment), duty of customs is levied at such rates as may be specified under Customs Tariff Act, 1975 on goods imported into, or exported from India. This is known as basic customs duty (BCD). It is levied under Section 12 of the Customs Act and specified under Section 2 of the Customs Tariff Act.

As per Section 2 of the Customs Tariff Act, the rates at which duties of customs shall be levied are indicated in the First Schedule and the Second Schedule of this Act. First Schedule deals with import tariff and Second Schedule with export tariff.

The duty may be a percentage of the value of the goods or at a specific rate. The Central Government has the power to reduce or exempt any goods from these duties.

BCD on imports indicates the *level of protection* which the Government wants to provide to domestic industries, subject to WTO rules, regulations and norms. [1]

IGST on imports ensures *level playing field* between imported goods and domestically produced goods.

In the pre-GST era, *level playing field* was ensured through Additional Duty of Customs [commonly known as

Countervailing Duty (CVD)] under Section 3(1) of the Customs Tariff Act, 1975, on goods imported into the country. The rate of this duty was equal to the excise duty on like articles if produced or manufactured in India. [2]

Similarly, Special Additional Duty of Customs (SAD), also known as Special CVD, was levied under Section 3(5) of the Customs Tariff Act, 1975. This duty was equal to sales tax/VAT, local taxes or any other charge on a like article on its sale, purchase or transportation in India. Again, the purpose of SAD was to counter balance various state level taxes and provide *level playing field* to indigenous goods which had to bear these taxes/charges.

With effect from July 1, 2017, these duties (CVD and Special CVD) were replaced by IGST. As already stated, the underlying philosophy of IGST is to endure *level playing field* between imported goods and domestically produced goods. In other words, IGST ensures that that the *level of protection* provided by the basic import duty (under Section 2 of the Customs Tariff Act, 1975) to domestic industry is not reduced.

15.5 Calculation of IGST

IGST is calculated on the aggregate of the following:

1. Assessable value.
2. Basic customs duty.
3. Social welfare surcharge (10 percent of basic customs duty).

15.5.1 Compensation Cess: It is a cess levied under Section 8 of the Goods and Services Tax (Compensation to States) Act, 2017. It is applicable—in addition to the regular GST taxes (CGST + SGST/UT-GST on intra-state supplies and IGST on inter-state supplies—on the supply of certain notified goods/services. The following goods—which mostly belong to the luxury and demerit categories—have been notified for the purpose so far.

1. *Pan masala.*
2. Tobacco and tobacco products.

3. Coal.
4. Aerated waters.
5. Motor vehicles.

The rate of compensation cess varies for different notified goods. It is imposed to compensate states for any revenue loss on account of implementation of GST.

In case compensation cess is applicable on goods imported into India, then it is levied and collected in accordance with the provisions of Section 3 of the Customs Tariff Act, 1975, at the point when duties of customs are levied on the said goods under Section 12 of the Customs Act, 1962, on a value determined under the Customs Tariff Act, 1975.

The cess is levied and collected along with customs duty and IGST.

15.6 Other Notable Points: These are as under:

1. IGST is applicable in case of import of goods/services.
2. IGST is not applicable on baggage.
3. Input tax credit pertaining to IGST paid is available.
4. If an exemption is given on inter-state supply under IGST Act, 2017, it is taken into consideration while calculating IGST for the purpose of import.

15.7 Exemptions from IGST on Certain Imports

At its Twenty-third Meeting held in Guwahati (Assam) on November 10, 2017, the GST Council took major decisions relating to GST rates, ITC eligibility criteria, and exemptions and clarifications on levy of GST on services. In the context of imports it approved the following exemptions:

1. Exemption from IGST on imports of lifesaving medicine supplied free of cost by overseas supplier for patients, subject to certification by DGHS of Centre or State and certain other conditions.
2. Exemption from IGST on imports of goods (other than motor vehicles) under a lease agreement if IGST is paid on the lease amount.

3. Exemption from IGST on imports of specified goods by a sports person of outstanding eminence, subject to specified conditions.
4. Exemption from GST on specified goods, such as scientific or technical instruments, software, and prototype supplied to public funded research institution or a university or IISc, or IITs or NIT.
5. Coverage of more items, such as temporary import of professional equipment by accredited press persons visiting India to cover certain events, broadcasting equipments, sports items, testing equipment, under ATA carnet system. These goods are to be re-exported after the specified use is over.

Endnotes

1. Apart from BCD, various other duties are also levied on imports, viz. anti-dumping duty, safeguard duty, protective duty, and social welfare surcharge. For details, see chapter 14 of this book.
2. **Additional (Countervailing) Duty of Customs:** The rate of this duty, popularly known as countervailing duty, was equal to the excise duty on like articles if produced or manufactured in India. If the rate of this duty was on *ad valorem* basis, the value for this purpose was the total of the value of the imported article and the customs duty on it (both basic and auxiliary). The underlying philosophy of a countervailing duty is to ensure that the protection provided by the import duty to domestic industry is not reduced. Till the early 1960s, countervailing duty was levied on a select basis on products which were considered to erode the margin of protection to the domestic industry on account of the excise duty. In course of time when the number of excisable goods increased, the selective use of countervailing duty was found to be inadequate and complicated. Therefore, the Indian Tariff Act, 1934, was amended in 1963 to insert a new Section 2A to provide for the levy of countervailing duty in all cases where excise duty was leviable on a similar indigenous commodity.

16

Dumping of Chinese Goods in India

16.1 What is Dumping?

It is a practice of selling goods in a foreign country at a price below their domestic selling price, after allowing for differences due to transportation expenses, tariffs, and other cost justifications. Many governments view the activity as an unfair competitive practice and frequently expose those engaged in dumping to the imposition of an antidumping duty. This generally unfavourable view of the practice stems from the monopoly precondition which underlies it. Economic theory specifies that in order for a producer to discriminate in the pricing of identical goods between markets (or classes of consumers) some element of monopoly power must be present; otherwise, the producer is merely a price-taker forced to adopt the uniform competitive price determined in the overall marketplace.

16.1.1 Conditions for Successful Dumping: For successful international dumping, the following conditions need to be satisfied.

1. The home and foreign markets are sufficiently separated to prevent arbitrage by foreign buyers in such a way that the cheap dumped goods cannot be resold by foreign buyers in the original market at a price which undercuts the domestic monopoly price.
2. There exists less competition in the home market than the foreign market, making foreign customers more responsive to an individual producer's price changes than domestic customers. Under these circumstances, the incentive for a producer to engage in international dumping is explained by the broader concept and theory of third-degree price discrimination, of which dumping is really a special case.

A producer interested in maximising profits given these conditions should price goods in different geographical locations so that the marginal revenue received from the last unit of those goods sold is equal in all locations, and at the same time equal to the overall marginal cost of production of those goods. If it is assumed that there is no difference in costs between markets and the revenue the producer receives from selling an additional unit of goods in the foreign market exceeds that received from the last unit sold in the home market, it is more profitable to lower the foreign price in order to sell another unit there and to raise the domestic price in order to sell a unit less at home. The incentive to re-price continues until the marginal revenues from each market are equilibrated to each other as well as to marginal cost of production. Where foreign market demand facing the producer is more responsive to price changes than domestic market demand, and where arbitrage cannot occur, this profit-maximising formula will ultimately result in a situation where the producer is motivated to price goods in the foreign market cheaper than at home.

Dumping duty is an additional import duty imposed to offset the effect of dumping which is found to materially injure the domestic industry.

16.2 Dumping of Chinese Goods in India

It is a well-known fact a large number of low priced shoddy/spurious products are coming from China to India. China is a very important trading partner for India. India has deep trade relations with China since the official resumption of trade with it in 1978. With China's accession to World Trade Organization (WTO) in December, 2001, our bilateral trade received a further impetus.

The increasing imports from China have taken its toll on our manufacturing sector. The Chinese goods have compelled many industrial units especially MSMEs to either operate at below its capacity or these have been forced to shut down. This has adversely affected local employment. The surge in imports from China has been on account of cheaper price it offers for a product. Though the quality of these products is often questionable but lack of awareness of Indian consumers have created a market for these products in India. There is an urgent need to educate and encourage the people about the importance of quality products and promote buying of Indian goods.

16.3 Why Chinese Goods are More Competitive than Indian Goods?

Chinese competitiveness is mainly the outcome of the efforts and support of the Chinese Government. China is not recognized by WTO as a market economy mainly because of the lack of transparency in its trade policy. A large number of companies which are dominant player in exports are Government- controlled enterprises.

While China has been long accused of manipulating its currency to maintain export competitiveness, it has also been found guilty of unfair trade practices like export subsidies that are in contravention to WTO regulations. The Committee was given to understand that Chinese Government gives export rebate to the tune of 17 percent to their exporters.

Further, regional provinces in China extend incentives and rebates on the tax structure and are competing with each other to attract industries in their region and also promoting exports by extending sizeable incentives (even on software downloads and logistics compensation for long distance freight) which makes Chinese products cost effective.

China accounts for the maximum number of anti-dumping duty/countervailing duty investigations around the world.

Apart from WTO non-compliant trade measures, Chinese competitiveness is also led by an enabling policy environment wherein the Government has made considerable interventions in ensuring that all the factors of production (land, labour, capital) are available at the cheapest cost to its manufacturers. The lending rates in China are very industry-friendly while in

India, the banks charge one of the highest lending rates from the industry. Our industry is borrowing anywhere between 11 and 14 percent while the Chinese are getting loans at 6 percent.

Chinese manufacturers are producing different qualities according to demand including cheap, but poor quality, products also. Such poor quality products are available at lower prices in Indian markets.

16.4 Adverse Consequences of Chinese Goods

Ever-increasing Chinese imports have played a negative role for the domestic industry. Industries that have been adversely affected by the import of Chinese goods are labour-intensive. These industries have traditionally been large employment generators in India (e.g. textiles) or are likely to become so (e.g. solar industry).

Downsizing or closing down of units in India will affect tax collections and impinge upon the 'Make in India' programme. Further, the closure of industry will also stress the banking sector which already is reeling under the burden of huge NPAs.

In addition to revenue and employment, low-quality Chinese imports also have an adverse impact on the environment. For instance, import of impure chemicals affects the environment, and results in low quality agrochemicals (pesticides) thus affecting Indian farmers. Poor quality toys, colours, firecrackers, statues of gods and goddesses, etc. from China, are health hazards in Indian household. Further, import dependence on China in some of the key products like bulk drugs on which our pharmaceutical industry is heavily dependent is quite worrisome.

The deluge of Chinese imports in the Indian market is wiping out many domestic industries and is a cause for serious concern. The methods adopted for dumping cheap Chinese goods in the Indian market include under-invoicing of goods, entry of prohibited Chinese goods by mis-declaration and outright smuggling.

India cannot ill afford such a situation. In fact, the problem of Chinese dumping is a matter of concern across the globe.

16.5 Anti-dumping and Other Trade Remedial Measures

Dumping occurs when one country (say China) exports an article to another country (say India) at a price lower than its normal value. Since this is an unfair trade practice having a disruptive effect on international trade, anti-dumping duty comes in handy as a measure to rectify the situation.

India has an elaborate and robust legal framework and institutional set up to protect its environment, life and health of its people, plants and animals. All goods imported into India are subject to domestic laws, rules, orders, regulations, technical specifications, environment and safety norms that are notified from time-to-time.

Both India and China are members of the WTO, therefore no restrictions can be imposed on trade if the same is WTO-compliant, i.e. there is no violation of domestic rules and regulations. However, in case the Government considers any measure as inconsistent with the WTO agreement and impacting India's trade interest, the matter is taken up at appropriate forum including the bilateral and multilateral forums (WTO Committee).

India does not have any bilateral trade agreement with China giving it preferential treatment. China has been accorded Most Favoured Nation (MFN) status [1] as envisaged for WTO Members States. The applicable rates of duties are thus charged on imports from China. Except approximately five hundred tariff lines which are either *restricted* or *prohibited* for import, all other goods are *free* for import, subject to these meeting/fulfilling other statutory requirements/stipulated conditions.

In addition, trade defence measures like anti-dumping duty and countervailing duty, safeguard measures are available to industries to seek remedies under the prescribed WTO provisions.

The trade remedial measures available to the trade and industry of the WTO member countries permissible under the WTO Agreement comprise of the following:

1. Anti-dumping measures.
2. Anti-subsidy measures (also known as countervailing measures).
3. Safeguard measures (tariff).
4. Safeguard measures (quantitative restrictions).

16.5.1 Anti-dumping Duty: Central Government can impose anti-dumping duty by issue of a notification under Section 9A of the Customs Tariff Act, 1975. However, anti-dumping duty cannot exceed *margin of dumping* in relation to such article. Margin of dumping means the difference between *normal value* and *export price*. Normal value means comparable price in ordinary course in trade, for like article, when destined for consumption in the exporting country. Export price means the price at which goods are exported.

Anti-dumping duty is generally imposed in cases where Indian production units are manufacturing similar articles.

It is noteworthy that Section 9B (1) (b) of Customs Tariff Act, 1975 provides restrictions on the power of the Government to impose anti-dumping duty in the case of imports from a WTO member country. In such cases, anti-dumping duty can be imposed only if the Central Government declares that import of such articles in India causes material injury to Industry established in India or materially retards the establishment of any industry in India.

Anti-dumping duty falls under the purview of Directorate General of Trade Remedies (DGTR) [earlier Directorate General of Anti-Dumping and Allied Duties (DGAD)]. Hence, anti-dumping duty investigations are carried out by DGTR. After detailed investigations, preliminary/final findings were issued by DGAD based on which, Department of Revenue imposed provisional/definitive anti-dumping duties.

DGAD conducted anti-dumping and CVD investigations on the basis of a duly substantiated application filed by the domestic industry alleging dumping or subsidization of goods into the country causing injury to the domestic industry. The proceedings were carried out in accordance with the relevant rules which were fully aligned and harmonious with WTO Agreement. These investigations were quasi-judicial in nature which had to be completed and final findings to be issued within 12 months from the date of initiation unless extended by another 6 months by the Government of India. To ensure timely completion of investigation, time lines for various stages of investigation have been laid down by the designated authority.

Above measures are not meant to ensure general economic protection to domestic industry per se but are imposed only to ensure a level playing field for the domestic industry to mitigate the injury caused to them due to unfair practices of dumping or subsidization. These measures are levied initially for a period up to 5 years.

16.6 Impact of Chinese Goods on Indian Industry

Presented below are the highlights of the Report of the Department Related Parliamentary Standing Committee on Commerce Presented to the Parliament on July 26, 2018.

1. India has been showing negative balance of trade in its bilateral trade with China. The trade deficit with China at US$ 63 billion in 2017-18 constituted more than 40 percent of India's total trade deficit.
2. During the period 2007-08 to 2017-18, there has been an increase in India's exports to China by US$ 2.5 billion; the imports, however, increased by US$ 50 billion during this period.
3. On enquiring about the status of trade remedial measures taken against China, the Committee was informed that India has highest number of anti-dumping investigations initiated against China. As on 27.12.2017, DGAD has initiated 864 anti-dumping investigations over 375 products since January, 1994. China is involved in anti-

dumping investigations for 214 products. In comparison, there are 86 anti-dumping cases initiated against EU, 64 cases against South Korea, 62 cases against Taiwan and 41 cases each against Japan and USA.

4. The Committee noted that as on April 18, 2018, definitive anti-dumping duty was in force on 144 products out of which 102 products pertained to China. Further, 24 more cases on imports from China were initiated.
5. The Committee also noted that currently, countervailing duty was in force on two products from China and one countervailing duty investigation against China was under progress. The DGAD also carried two anti-circumvention investigations during last three years.
6. The Committee thus noted that China faces the major chunk of anti-dumping investigations which is a clear indication that Chinese goods are causing unfair trade disruption. The Committee during its deliberation with industry noted that present state of anti-dumping investigations against the Chinese goods was not the actual reflection of the problem of unfair trade being faced by Indian Industry, especially, MSME Sector. The problem runs deep and all the industries affected by the dumping are not able to reach DGAD on account of high cost involved in moving the application. It was informed that the application process for initiating anti-dumping and other trade defence measures was a costly affair and not easily affordable for the SMEs. It was also pointed out that the investigation being undertaken by DGAD are protracted and by the time the duty is notified, the injury caused to the domestic industry leaves it weak and bleeding forever.
7. The Committee appreciates that there is a move towards shortening the time period of completing the investigations in 270 days from the present 365 days and reduce the period from 90 days to 30 days for Tax Research Unit in Department of Revenue to accept and issue the

Notification. The Committee feels that this period may further be reduced to 180 days and 15 days respectively so that damages to domestic industry may be contained in right earnest.

8. The anti-dumping framework suffers from lax implementation. The unscrupulous elements are able to import the Chinese goods by circumventing the goods put under anti-dumping framework through misclassification of products. This mis-declaration while importing the goods which otherwise have been put under anti-dumping measures nullify the whole effort to protect the domestic industry from unfair trade practices.
9. The Committee finds that while anti-dumping measures are being evaded on the one hand proving it to be ineffective; on the other hand, there is a general reluctance on the part of the Government to review the effectiveness of anti dumping measures undertaken by it. Rather there is no provision to carry out any impact assessment of the anti-dumping duty/countervailing duty imposed by DGAD.
10. The Committee expresses its deep concern over lax implementation of law since it makes the problem to persist and domestic industry suffers in the form of shutdown of the units and loss of employment. One estimate suggests that due to the dumping of Chinese solar panel there is a loss of nearly two lakh jobs as nearly half of our domestic industry capacity remains idle. This is something that the Committee finds shocking. It strongly recommends the Department to address the problem of poor implementation of DGAD findings on dumping and subsidy of Chinese goods.
11. The Committee was further informed that the problem of flooding of Chinese goods goes beyond mere dumping. The unscrupulous imports from China are also on account of influx of under-invoiced Chinese goods, goods brought in through mis-declaration and outright smuggling. These

illegalities have its share of adverse effect on Indian industry. There is a real challenge to maintain a very fine balance between trade facilitation and enforcement.

12. During the year 2017-18, total anti-dumping duty (ADD) of ₹ 1,268 crore was collected, out of this anti-dumping duty of ₹ 798 crore was collected from the goods imported from China, which is 63 percent of total ADD collection.
13. It discovered that since many Chinese goods like toys are not subject to mandatory quality standards, the Indian market is flooded with poor quality toys many of which contain harmful chemicals and materials. Similarly, it was informed that the Indian market is flooded with poor quality made in China LED bulbs. It was brought to the notice of the Committee that as per one study, 50-70 percent light bulbs and fixtures are spurious and sub-standard and these are predominantly Chinese products.
14. The Committee found that many factors have gone into making China a competitive producer of goods and pose as an aggressive trading nation globally. While the companies in China enjoy the benefit of huge physical infrastructural and logistic advantage, easy access to low-interest finance, economy in scale of production, integration to global value chain, control and supply of raw materials, skilled workforce, etc. which make them competitive, the Chinese industry has also been benefited by opaque government interventions to boost low cost production, manipulated currency (though there has been an appreciation in the value of Chinese currency in recent past) to make Chinese export competitive, handing out of WTO non-compliant export subsidies, provisioning of special incentives to boost exports, IP misappropriation, etc. The effect of this legitimate and illegitimate support has helped China create huge inventory of products and dump their products globally. The Committee finds that India has been an easy dumping ground for Chinese goods on 50 account of low price of Chinese goods, poor

enforcement and porous border both at sea and land.

15. There has been huge outrage globally to illegitimate Chinese trade practices and injury being caused to the local industry by dumping of Chinese goods and ever rising trade deficit. The concerns have been so deep that the United States has issued two Executive Orders to address the problem of rising trade deficit with China.
16. While the United States and the European Union have been quite aggressive and agitated over the erosion of their domestic industry and loss of employment, the Committee feels that Government should be more proactive in taking trade defence measures as provided by WTO and imposition of other trade restrictions on import of such Chinese goods which have caused erosion of our manufacturing capacity.
17. The impact of Chinese imports has been such that India is threatened to become a country of importers and traders with domestic factories either cutting down their 52 production or shutting down completely.
18. Refund of IGST on exports need to be cured at the earliest. Further, low-interest loans still continue to elude the industry.

Endnote

1. **Most Favoured Nation (MFN) Clause:** MFN clause is at the heart of modern commercial diplomacy. Under it, parties give each other all of the concessions which they give to any other country. The nomenclature is somewhat misleading as it sounds like a promise of preferential treatment. Instead, it is a promise that *no other country* will be given preferential treatment. In other words, the partner will receive treatment no less favourable than that given to any other country.

17

India and World Trade Organization (WTO)

17.1 Establishment of WTO

Created by Uruguay Round of Negotiations (1986-94), WTO was established on January 1, 1995 with headquarters in Geneva, Switzerland. As on June 1, 2020, 164 countries of the world were members of WTO. WTO's creation in 1995 marked the biggest reform of international trade since 1948. During those 47 years, international commerce was regulated under General Agreement on Tariffs and Trade (GATT) which helped establish a prosperous multilateral trading system. However, by the end of 1980s an overhaul was due.

The Eighth Round of multilateral trade negotiations held under GATT and named Uruguay Round, resulted in new legal agreements for trade and strengthening settlement system. Following this, there was a Ministerial Conference in Marrakesh, Morocco in April 1994 attended by 125 government representatives from across the world to sign for the establishment of a new successor institution of GATT, namely the World Trade Organization (WTO). WTO entered into force on January 1, 1995, with all assets and liabilities of GATT transferred to the former. WTO replaced GATT which remained in existence from 1948 to 1994. GATT was a multilateral treaty, governing trade in goods only. WTO is much wider in scope and coverage.

The Uruguay Round was the largest trade negotiations ever. At times the talks seemed doomed to fail, but in the end the Uruguay Round was successful. The task was so immense that some people wondered whether there would ever be another negotiations like these. Was it the round to end all rounds?

WTO is GATT plus a lot more. GATT (the institution) was small and provisional, and not even recognised in law as international organisation. It was replaced by WTO. GATT (the agreement) was amended and incorporated into the new WTO Agreements. GATT dealt only with trade in goods. WTO Agreements cover services and intellectual property as well.

WTO is the only international body dealing with the rules of trade between nations. At its heart are the WTO agreements, the legal ground rules for international commerce and for trade policy. The agreements have three main objectives: (a) to help trade flow as freely as possible, (b) to achieve further liberalisation gradually through negotiations and (c) to set up an impartial means of settling disputes.

A number of simple, fundamental principles run throughout all the WTO agreements. They are the foundation of the multilateral trading system. They include: non-discrimination, freer trade, predictable policies, encouragement to competition and extra provisions for less developed countries.

The economic case for an open trading system based on multilaterally agreed rules is simple enough and rests largely on commercial common sense. Protectionism leads to bloated inefficient companies and can in the end lead to factory closures and job losses. One of the WTO's objectives is to reduce protectionism.

Broadly speaking, WTO has set to continue negotiations and bring agreements in the following areas.

1. Basic telecommunications.
2. Maritime transport.
3. Movement of natural persons.
4. Financial services.
5. General Agreement on Trade and Services (GATS).
6. A reaffirmation of the rule of law in trade and economic relations.
7. A reversal of long standing protectionist practices in agriculture, textiles and clothing.
8. An extension of multilateral rules to services and intellectual property rights.

WTO is run by its member governments. All major decisions are made by the membership as a whole, either by ministers (who meet every two years) or by officials (who meet regularly in Geneva). Decisions are normally taken by consensus. More routine work is supervised by the General Council. Numerous other councils, committees, working parties and negotiating groups cover the wide range of WTO issues.

WTO is directed by a Ministerial Conference which is the highest authority and meets at least once every two years. So far, 11 Ministerial Conferences have been held, namely in Singapore (December 1996), Geneva (May 1998), Seattle (November-December 1999), Doha (November 2001), Cancun (September 2003), Hong Kong (December 2005), Geneva (November-December 2009), Geneva (December 2011), Bali (December 2013, Nairobi (December 2015), Buenos Aires (December 2017). The 12th Ministerial Conference is proposed to be held in Nur-Sultan in June 2021.

WTO is based on the principles of non-discrimination, free trade and promotion of fair competition among the member countries. About 95 percent of the global trade is governed by the rules and regulations of WTO. WTO agreements are permanent and ratified by the Parliaments of member countries.

17.2 Trade Policy Reviews (TPRs) of India

In order to promote transparency and provide better understanding of the trade policies and practices of its Members, the World Trade Organization (WTO) has a mechanism for regular review of their trade policies. TPR provides the country under review a feedback on its performance in the WTO system. For this purpose, the WTO Secretariat prepares a detailed report on the trade policies and practices of the country under review (Secretariat Report), which is supplemented by a policy statement of the Government under review (Government Report). These two reports form the basis for the review, and are public documents, available on WTO website.

The TPR offers opportunity to other WTO Members to ask questions and raise concerns on different aspects of policies and practices of the country under review. These written advance questions, generally based on the contents of the Secretariat Report and the Government Report, are required to be replied in writing by start of the review meeting.

Depending upon its share in world trade, each Member's trade policy is reviewed by the WTO at fixed periodic intervals. India's Trade Policy Review is carried out every 4 years.

17.2.1 Fifth Trade Policy Review (TPR) of India: The Fifth TPR of India was held on September 14 and 16, 2011 at WTO, Geneva. Before the meeting, the WTO Secretariat circulated a compilation of India's written replies to 886 advance questions raised by 26 WTO Members. Replying to these questions required co-ordination involving almost 70 Departments and Ministries of the Government of India.

On September 14, 2011, the proceedings started with the introductory remarks of the Chairperson of the TPRB (Trade Policy Review Body). This was followed by the opening statement of the Commerce Secretary, who led the Indian delegation, giving an overview of policies and new developments. Thereafter, the Discussant spoke on main issues covered in the WTO Secretariat Report and the Government Report. The subsequent proceedings witnessed oral interventions from 42 WTO Members.

During the review, most of the Members commended the resilience of Indian economy that smoothly withstood the adverse effects of global financial crisis without taking recourse to protectionist measures. Members appreciated India for using its trade policy to promote sustainable development and inclusive growth. Members also noted India's positive engagement in Doha Round negotiations. Some of the Members, notably US, raised concerns in certain areas, viz. tariffs and duties; licensing and restrictions; trade defence measures (anti-dumping), Government procurement, incentives schemes to promote investments and exports, tariff protection on agriculture, services and investments.

Following responses to the issues raised were provided in India's Closing Statement on September 16, 2011.

1. **Openness of India's Trading Regime:** Questions were asked about the openness of India's trading regime. In response India pointed out that year after year, India's imports had outpaced exports. In terms of percentage of GDP, the country's merchandise trade deficit is one of the highest in the world. India has been autonomously reducing its tariffs over the years. The simple average most favoured nation (MFN) tariff rate declined from 15.1 percent in 2006-7 to 12 percent in 2010-11. The tariffs on 71 percent of India's tariff lines are between 5 and 10 percent.
2. **Gap between India's Bound and Applied Rates on Agricultural Products:** Some members mentioned the large gap between India's bound and applied rates on agricultural products. India responded that the large gap reflected India's steady and continued autonomous tariff liberalization. During the 4 years since the last TPR, the tariffs on some agricultural commodities had to be adjusted in the face of high volatility in food prices. In most cases tariffs have been brought down and have stayed down. In a few instances they have been raised again but never above their original levels.
3. **Export Incentives:** Questions were asked about export promotion schemes. It was explained that India's export promotion schemes are based on the concept of duty neutralization and providing a level playing field. These schemes are reviewed regularly.
4. **FDI Policy:** To a number of questions on FDI policy, India explained that the continuing thrust, during the period since India's last TPR in 2007, has been on making the FDI policy more liberal and investment-friendly. The FDI guidelines have been significantly rationalized, simplified, and consolidated, with the aim of providing a single policy platform for reference of foreign investors. Several new sectors such as petroleum and natural gas and

civil aviation were either opened up to foreign investment or significantly liberalized during this period. Efforts were also being made to streamline and simplify the business environment and make regulations conducive to business.

5. **Intellectual Property (IP) Policies and Enforcement:** On questions related to India's IP policies, India replied that a number of initiatives have been taken to enhance IP protection and enforcement. The changes proposed in the Copyright and Trademark Acts would enhance protection to intellectual property rights (IPRs) in digital technology, particularly with regard to the dissemination of protected material over digital networks. These have been supplemented by administrative as well as judicial measures to strengthen the IPR regime. The provisions on IP protection in these laws are further supplemented by border measures to prevent the import of goods involving copyright piracy and counterfeit trademarks. Another initiative taken by Indian customs is the facility for online registration by the right holders through the web-based Automatic Recordation and Targeting for IPR Protection System.
6. **Government Procurement:** On this subject, India explained that the procurement of high tech items and high value tenders, above US$ 50,000, is generally open to international bidders. Major reforms are on the anvil for increasing coverage, improving transparency and efficiency, and better enforcement, which are triggered by domestic concerns relating to enhancing the value for money. An omnibus procurement law applicable to the entire country and to all procuring entities, including public-sector enterprises, is being deliberated upon.
7. **Sanitary and Phyto-sanitary (SPS) and Technical Barriers to Trade (TBT) Measures:** In response to question on SPS and TBT measures, India explained that specific trade concerns raised against India have been largely addressed. Regulations adopted in the past have been on the basis of scientific risk analysis.

8. **Export Restrictions:** There were some questions on India's use of export restrictions. India responded that export restrictions have been used on some occasions for purposes of domestic supply management but these have been purely on a temporary basis. The ban on the export of rice and wheat had to be extended in 2009 due to a dislocation in production and again in 2010 due to the severest drought in the country in the last 40 years. However, the export of wheat and non-basmati rice is now completely free. The export of basmati rice is and has always been free. Restrictions on cotton exports were imposed for only a brief period last year. Cotton yarn exports have been made completely free. Similarly, cotton is also freely exportable.
9. **Other Issues:** There were questions related to customs valuation, tariffs, and other charges, internal taxation, import licensing, and the use of trade remedies. In response, it was pointed out that India cannot be accused of protectionist intent in its use of trade remedies. If that were the case, then the easy route of increasing the tariffs up to the bound rates could have been used; that has not been done. Anti-dumping measures are legitimate instruments against unfair trade practices.
10. Investigations are carried out in a fair and transparent manner and subjected to strict scrutiny. As a rule India only imposes the lesser duty and not the full dumping margin as is done by some WTO members. This underscores the fact that trade remedies are not used as a protectionist tool.

Despite the fact that many members, with very deep pockets, use subsidies as part of their trade policy, India has not imposed a single anti-subsidy measure. As on date, there is only one safeguard duty in force. In the wake of the economic crisis, there was a spurt in application of safeguard investigations in 2009. A total of 14 applications were received but in 9 cases, investigations were either terminated or a decision was taken not to impose any safeguard duty. Duties were imposed only in 5 cases and those too have since been withdrawn. Moreover, India has never taken recourse to quantitative restrictions as safeguard measures. Import licensing affects only a few restricted items primarily on grounds of protection of human, animal, and plant life and the environment. The licensing regime is open and transparent. Licences are granted on a non-discriminatory basis. The relevant regulations are all available in the public domain and the Directorate General of Foreign Trade (DGFT) acts as the nodal agency.

17.2.2 Sixth Trade Policy Review (TPR) of India: The Sixth TPR of India was held on April 28, 2015 at WTO, Geneva. Following are the observations from the Report prepared by the WTO Secretariat.

"During the period under review, India continued its efforts to liberalize and facilitate trade, such as through the introduction of self-assessment in customs procedures and the elimination of state-trading requirements for some agricultural products. India also proceeded with further structural reforms including by eliminating price controls on diesel and relaxing foreign direct investment (FDI) restrictions in some sectors. Nonetheless, the tariff structure remains complex and the simple average MFN tariff rate increased during the review period.

India has continued its process of fiscal consolidation. Nonetheless, throughout the review period, India continued to post sizeable public sector deficits. According to India's regulations, the Government is required to reduce its fiscal deficit to 3 percent by 2017-18. It also intends to further streamline taxes including by introducing a goods and services tax (GST).

As recognized by the Government, structural bottlenecks remain a barrier to achieve a higher growth. This includes delays in project approval, ill-targeted subsidies, low manufacturing base and low agricultural productivity, difficulty in land acquisition, weak transportation network and power supply, and strict labour regulations and skill mismatches. These bottlenecks are being addressed through investment in infrastructure and education, simplification of the business environment by eliminating overregulation, and increasing predictability in trade and investment regimes.

Measures to attract FDI have included gradually increasing the number of sectors in which FDI is permitted and reducing sectoral restrictions. Since its last Review, India has continued to liberalize its investment policies, including raising foreign-ownership limits in some sectors, such as insurance and railway transport.

India is one of the most active users of anti-dumping measures among WTO Members; it initiated more than 80 anti-dumping investigations against 23 trading partners during the period under review. During the same period, significant changes were made to India's anti-dumping legislation including new rules defining situations that are considered to represent the circumvention of anti-dumping duties, and providing for anti-circumvention investigations to address such circumvention. India initiated one countervailing investigation during the period; no definitive countervailing measure is in place. Since its last Review, India has also initiated 18 safeguard investigations.

Since its last Review, India has taken several initiatives to modernize its IPR administration and continue its efforts to enforce IPRs. The Copyright Act was amended, *inter alia*, to implement the 1996 WIPO Copyright Treaty and guidelines were issued on patents for biological materials, both in 2012. In March 2012, India issued its first and only compulsory licence (on certain anti-cancer medicines).

The Government also launched a "Make in India" campaign in 2014 to strengthen the sector and attract investment".

Bibliography

Bibliography

A.T. Kearney, Inc. (2001), Global Business Policy Council, "FDI Confidence Audit: India", Alexandria, Virginia, USA.

Acharya, Shankar N. (1999), "Managing External Economic Challenges in the Nineties: Lessons for the Future", 18th Anniversary Lecture of the Centre for Banking Studies, Central Bank of Sri Lanka, Occasional Paper No. 33, ICRIER.

Adndre, Sapir (1983), "Factors Influencing India's Export Performance", Indian Council for Research and International Economic Relations, New Delhi, Working Paper No. 9.

Ahluwalia, Isher Judge (1991), "Productivity and Growth in Indian Manufacturing", London: Oxford University Press.

Alagh, K.Y. (1998), "Agricultural Trade and Policies", *Indian Economic Journal*, January-March.

Asian Development Bank (1987), "Towards Regional Co-operation in South Asia", Manila: Economics and Development Research Centre.

Balakrishnan, P., K. Pushpangadan and M. Suresh Babu (2000), "Trade Liberalisation and Productivity Growth in Manufacturing: Evidence from Firm Level Panel Data", *Economic and Political Weekly,* October.

Chand, S. and K. Sen (2002), "Trade Liberalisation and Productivity Growth: Evidence from Indian Manufacturing", *Review of Development Economics,* February, Volume 6, No. 1.

Chatterjee, Debojyoti (1993)," Hardsell for Software Exports", *Business Standard*, November 28.

Das, Deb Kusum (2002), "Trade Liberalisation and Industrial Productivity: An Assessment of Developing Country Experiences", ICRIER Working Paper No. 77.

Dholakia, R.H. and D. Kapur (2001), "Economic Reforms and Trade Performance: Private Corporate Sector in India", *Economic and Political Weekly*, Volume 36, No. 49, December.

Export-Import Bank of India (1991), "How Import Intensive are Indian Exports", Occasional Paper No. 16, December.

Feldstein, Martin (2000), "Aspects of Global Economic Integration: Outlook for the Future", National Bureau of Economic Research Working Paper No. 7899.

Goldar, B.N. and A. Kumari (2002), "Import Liberalisation and Productivity Growth in Indian Manufacturing Industries in the 1990s", Working Paper E/219, Institute of Economic Growth, Delhi.

Government of India, *Economic Survey* (various years).

—Ministry of Commerce and Industry, *Annual Report* (various years).

—Ministry of Finance, *Budget Papers* (various years).

—Ministry of Finance, High Level Committee on Balance of Payments (Chairman: C. Rangarajan), 1993.

—Planning Commission, Various Plan Documents.

—Report of the Committee on Import-Export Policies and Procedures" (Chairman: P. C. Alexander), New Delhi, 1978.

Gulati, Ashok and Tim Kelly (1999), "Trade Liberalization and Indian Agriculture", New Delhi: Oxford University Press.

Gulati, Ashok and Anil Sharma (1994), "Agriculture under GATT: What it Holds for India?", *Economic and Political Weekly*, Volume 29, No. 29.

Gulati, Ashok et al. (1994), "Export Competitiveness of Selected Agricultural Commodities", New Delhi: National Council of Applied Economic Research (NCAER).

Indian Institute of Foreign Trade (1998), "Global Economic Challenges in the New Millennium", New Delhi.

International Monetary Fund, "Balance of Payments Manual", Washington, D.C., 1977.

—*World Economic Outlook* (various issues).

Jalan, Bimal, "Exchange Rate Management: An Emerging Consensus", *RBI Bulletin*, September 2003.

— "International Financial Architecture: Developing Countries", *RBI Bulletin*, October 1999.

— "Monetary and Credit Policies", *RBI Bulletin*, April 2001.

Kapur, D. and U.R. Patel (2003), "Large Foreign Currency Reserves: Insurance for Domestic Weaknesses and External Uncertainties", *Economic and Political Weekly*, March.

Kesavan, K.V. (2001), (ed.), "Economic Liberalization in India: Japanese and Indian Perspectives", Delhi: Indian Council of Social Science Research.

Krishna, P. and D. Mitra (1998), "Trade Liberalisation, Market Discipline and Productivity Growth: New Evidence from India", *Journal of Development Economics*, August.

Lee, Jang-Yung (1996), "Implications of Surge in Capital Inflows:

Available Tools and Consequences for the Conduct of Monetary Policy", IMF Working Paper No. 43, May.

Lopez-Mejia, Alejandro (1999), "Large Capital Flows: A Survey of the Causes, Consequences, and Policy Responses", IMF Working Paper No. 17, February.

Mani, S. (1991), "External Liberalisation and Import-Dependence: A Note", *Economic and Political Weekly*, July.

Nayyar, Deepak and Abhijit Sen (1994), "International Trade and the Agricultural Sector in India", *Economic and Political Weekly*, May 14.

Organisation for Economic Co-operation and Development (2003), "OECD Code of Liberalisation of Capital Movements", OECD, March.

Patra, M.D. and S. Pattanaik (1994), "Exchange Rate Pass through Trade Balance: The Indian Experience", RBI Occasional Papers, Volume 15, No. 4.

Pattnaik, R.K., M. Kapur and S.C. Dhal (2003), "Exchange Rate Policy and Management: An Assessment of the Indian Experience", *Economic and Political Weekly*, Volume 38, No. 22.

Prabhu, P.P. (1998), "India's Trade Policy, New Delhi: Indian Institute of Foreign Trade.

Prasad, S. Eswar, Kenneth Rogoff, Shang-Jin Wei and M. Ayan Kose (2003), "Effects of Financial Globalisation on Developing Countries: Some Empirical Evidence", IMF Occasional Paper No. 220, September.

Rangarajan, C. and A. Prasad (1999), "Capital Account Liberalisation and Controls: Lessons from the East Asian Crisis", *ICRA Bulletin on Money and Finance*, No. 9, June.

Ranjan, Rajiv and M.D. Patra, "The Structure of India's Imports 1970-71 to 1988-89", RBI Occasional Papers, June 1992.

— "Competitiveness of India's Exports", RBI Occasional Papers, December 1995.

Reddy, Y.V., "Asian Crises: Asking Right Questions", *RBI Bulletin*, July 1998.

—"India's Foreign Exchange Reserves: Policy, Status and Issues", *RBI Bulletin*, July 2002.

Reserve Bank of India, "Report of the Committee on Capital Account Convertibility", (Chairman: S. S. Tarapore), 1997.

—*Report on Currency and Finance* (various years).

—*Handbook of Statistics on Indian Economy* (various years).

Sathe, D. (1997), "Import Intensity of India's Exports: Some Fresh Evidence", *Economic and Political Weekly*, February.

Sharma, Pardeep and Ashok Gulati (1995), "WTO and Indian Agriculture", *Economic and Political Weekly*, March 10.

Singh, Ajit and Jayati Ghosh (1988), "Import liberalisation and New Industrialisation Strategy: An Analysis of their Impact on Output and Employment in Indian Economy", *Economic and Political Weekly*, Volume 23, No. 45.

Singh, D.R. (1983), "Proxy Effects of Market in India's Exports", *Indian Economic Journal*, January-March.

Singh, Tarlok (2002), "India's Trade Balance: The Role of Income and Exchange Rates", *Journal of Policy Modelling*, Volume 24.

Tarapore, S.S. (2003), "Capital Account Convertibility: Monetary Policy and Reforms", New Delhi: UBS Publishers Distributors.

United Nations Conference on Trade and Development (UNCTAD),

—*World Investment Report* (various issues).

—*Trade and Development Report* (various issues).

—*World Investment Report* (various years).

Varma, M.L. (1990), "Exports of Gems and Jewellery: New Challenges", *Foreign Trade Bulletin*, Volume XXI, No. 6, December.

World Bank, *World Development Report* (various issues).

Yamazawa, Ippei (2000), "Developing Economies in the Twenty-First Century: The Challenge of Globalisation", Institute of Developing Economies, Japan.

Websites

Ministry of Commerce and Industry
Ministry of Finance
Reserve Bank of India
Confederation of Indian Industry (CII)
Federation of Indian Chambers of Commerce and Industry (FICCI)
NITI Aayog

Index

Index